POSSUMS

AUSTRALIAN NATURAL HISTORY SERIES

Series Editor: Professor Terence J. Dawson

The function of this series of titles is to make accessible accurate scientific information, complemented by high quality illustrations, on a wide variety of Australian animals. Written and illustrated by trained researchers and scientists, the series is intended for students and biologists at both secondary and tertiary levels and, in general, for readers with a serious interest in animals and the environment. Interested authors should contact UNSW Press or Professor Dawson, School of Biological Science, University of New South Wales, UNSW Sydney, NSW 2052.

Books published in the series:

Echidnas of Australia and New Guinea, Mike Augee & Brett Gooden
Illustrated by Anne Musser

Flying Foxes, Fruit and Blossom Bats of Australia by Leslie Hall & Greg Richards
Illustrated by Louise Saunders.

Goannas: The Biology of Varanid Lizards (2nd edition), Dennis King & Brian Green
Illustrated by Frank Knight, Keith Newgrain & Jo Eberhard

Kangaroos: Biology of the Largest Marsupials, Terence J. Dawson
Illustrated by Anne Musser and Jillian Hallam

The Koala: Natural History, Conservation and Management, Roger Martin & Kathrine Handasyde
Illustrated by Sue Simpson

Little Penguin: Fairy Penguins in Australia, Colin Stahel & Rosemary Gales
Illustrated by Jane Burrell

The Mountain Pygmy-possum of the Australian Alps, Ian Mansergh & Linda Broome
Illustrated by Katrina Sandiford

The Platypus: A Unique Mammal (2nd edition), Tom Grant
Illustrated by Dominic Fanning

Pythons of Australia: A Natural History, Geordie Torr
Illustrated by Eleanor Torr

Sea Snakes, Harold Heatwole

The Wombat: Common Wombats in Australia, Barbara Triggs
Illustrated by Ross Goldingay

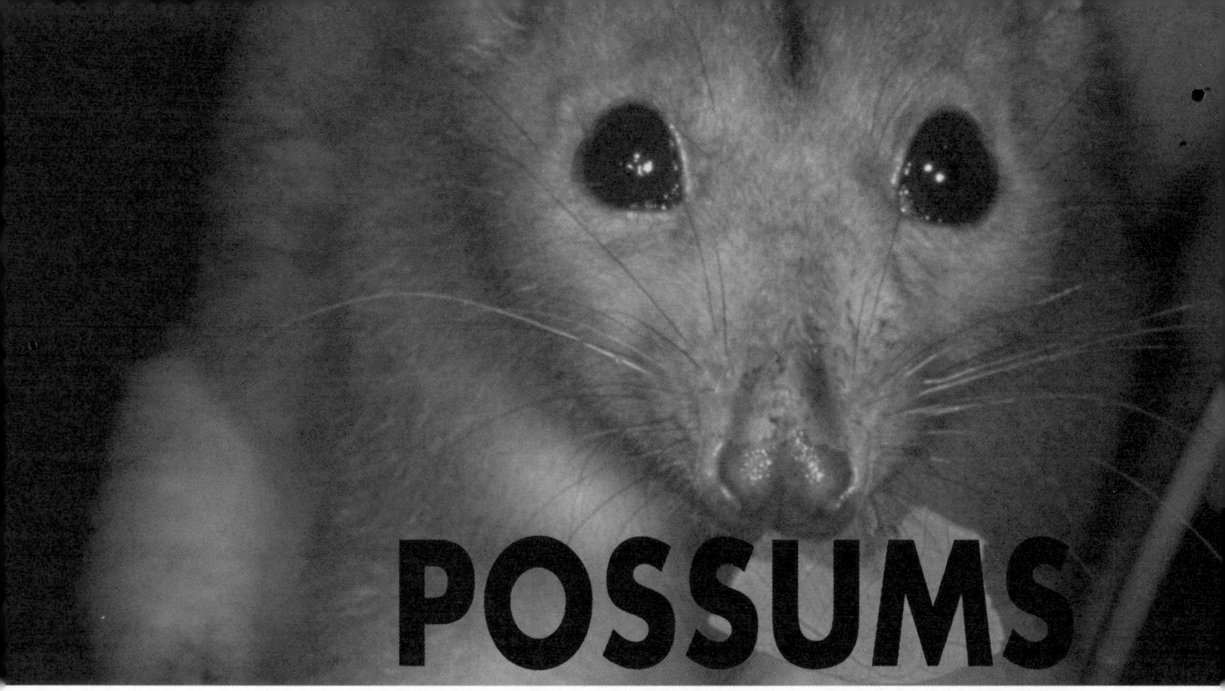

POSSUMS

THE BRUSHTAILS, RINGTAILS AND GREATER GLIDER

Anne Kerle

Illustrations by Veronica Saunders

UNSW PRESS

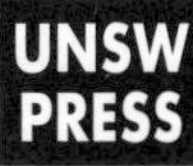

A UNSW Press book

Published by
University of New South Wales Press Ltd
University of New South Wales
UNSW Sydney NSW 2052
AUSTRALIA
www.unswpress.com.au

First published 2001

National Library of Australia
Cataloguing-in-Publication entry:

Kerle, J. Anne (Jean Anne)
Possums: the brushtails, ringtails and greater glider.

Includes index.
ISBN 0 86840 419 5.

1. Gliders (Mammals). 2. Phalangeridae. 3. Pseudocheiridae
I. Title. (Series: Australian natural history series).

599.23

Printer BPA, Melbourne

CONTENTS

PREFACE

Possums have been around me for as long as I can remember. The association began in my childhood with their unpopular raids on our roses and almond tree. I grew up in country New South Wales, surrounded by a love of nature which originated with my grandfather and was passed on through my parents. It was logical to pursue a career in biology.

My research into these wonderful animals began by accident. I planned to study rodent behaviour for my Honours project but couldn't get the species I wanted so, George McKay (my supervisor) suggested I work with the Mountain Pygmy Possums from Taronga Zoo. It was an excellent suggestion. I later travelled to the Top End of the Northern Territory planning a general ecological study for my PhD research but the Northern Brushtail Possums provided a much more interesting subject. This really opened the door into marsupial research and especially possum research with the guidance of Professor Geoff Sharman, a founder of marsupial research. Later I moved to central Australia where the 'Common' Brushtail is an endangered species and the Aboriginal custodians want them reintroduced to Uluru. That was the beginning of another fascinating phase of possum research for me. I am indebted to Geoff Sharman, George McKay, Barry Fox and Jeff Foulkes for all their wisdom, encouragement and support for each of these studies. Now I live and work in the central west of NSW where I frequently hear of the 'possums that used to be here'.

Writing this book has provided an overdue opportunity to synthesise and interpret all the information about the biology of the Australian species of the Phalangeridae and Pseudocheiridae. Some important themes have emerged: the common and 'well-known' species may not be so well-known or secure throughout their range as is generally thought; there is a great deal of ecological variation between populations and much more information is needed before we can be sure that they are being managed appropriately; we can't continue to rely on research from New Zealand to understand the Common Brushtail Possum in its natural habitat; we don't even know important details such as the gestation period of the Greater Glider, an apparently common species; and we still know very little about the remote and uncommon species. Much more research is needed.

The results of my own research are only a very small portion of the information I have drawn from to write this book. Much of the research is acknowledged in the bibliography but this is not an exhaustive list. I wish to thank these many colleagues. John Winter and Ric How deserve special mention for their long-term interest in the biology and conservation of these possums.

Permission to reproduce text, diagrams and photos has been generously provided by Anne Fairbairn for her grandfather's description of the crash of possum populations in the St George area; John Winter for the drawings of brushtail behaviour and the cross-section of the larynx; Geoff Sharman for the drawings of the newborn brushtail and the female reproductive tract; Ric How for photos; the Mitchell Library for the 1813 paintings of Aboriginal people hunting by John Heaviside Clark; HarperCollins Publishers for the plate by Neville Cayley and text from Ellis Troughton's *Furred Animals of Australia*; and Manaaki Whenua Press for the distribution map of the Brushtail Possum in New Zealand. The distribution maps, tracks and scats in Chapter 4 are mostly redrawn from 'The Mammals of Australia' (ed. R. Strahan 1995) and Barbara Triggs' valuable book *Tracks, Scats and Other Traces*. Norm McKenzie provided the distribution maps of the Rock Ringtail Possum and the Western Ringtail Possum.

The production of a book like this never happens without a great deal of support from many people. I especially wish to thank Veronica Saunders for her excellent drawings and diagrams; Gary Saunders for his critical artistic assessment; Mike Fleming for his many hours helping to produce the figures; Murray Ellis for access to his extensive personal journal library; Sandy Ingleby (Australian Museum) for the loan of possum skulls; Bill Foley for assistance with the feeding chapter; and John Elliot from UNSW Press for his patience and encouragement.

Most of all I want to acknowledge the unconditional support from my husband, Mike Fleming, who was also a most valuable sounding board for the contents of the book, and from my daughters Catharine and Alison.

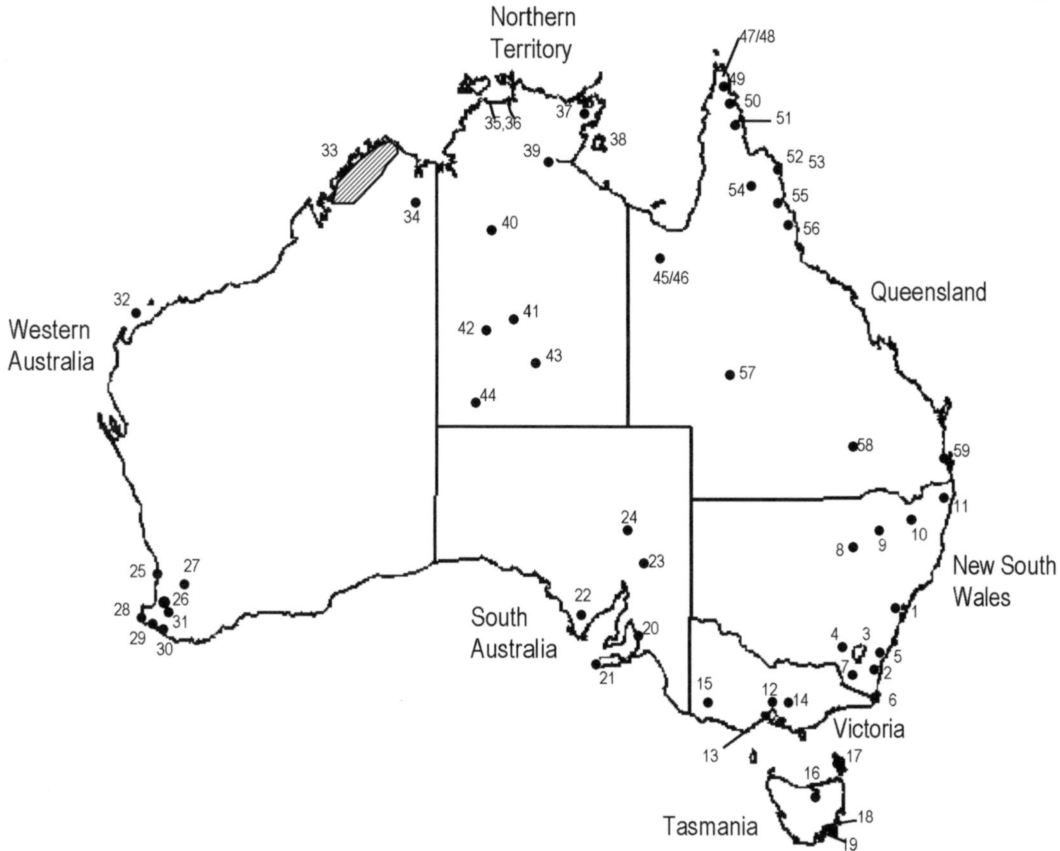

New South Wales & ACT
1. Sydney
2. Batemans Bay
2. Kioloa
3. Queanbeyan
4. Tumut
5. Bega
6. Eden
7. Coolangubra
8. Pilliga Forest
9. Armidale
10. Clouds Creek
11. Tweed River

Victoria
12. Melbourne/ Warramate Hills
13. Port Phillip Bay
14. Cambarville
15. Hamilton

Tasmania
16. Launceston
17. Flinders Island
18. Geeveston
19. Adventure Bay

South Australia
20. Adelaide
21. Kangaroo Island
22. Eyre Peninsula
23. Lake Frome
24. Lake Eyre

Western Australia
25. Perth
26. Burnie
27. Collie
28. Busselton
29. D'Entrecasteau Islands
30. Albany
31. Manjimup/Perup
32. Barrow Island
33. Kimberley
34. Turkey Creek

Northern Territory
35. Mary River NT
36. South Alligator River
37. Arnhemland
38. Groote Eylandt
39. Katherine & Roper Rivers
40. Lajamanu
41. Napperby
42. Haasts Bluff
43. Alice Springs
44. Uluru National Park

Queensland
45. Lawn Hill National Park
46. Riversleigh
47. Cape York
47. Lockerbie Scrub
48. Jardine River
49. Iron Range
50. McIlwraith Range
51. Coen
52. Mossman
53. Cairns
53. Bellenden Ker Range
54. Atherton Tableland
55. Cardwell
55. Herbert River
55. Ingham
56. Townsville
57. Mount Windsor Tableland
58. St George
59. Brisbane

CHAPTER 1

THE BRUSHTAIL AND RINGTAIL POSSUMS AND THEIR RELATIVES

'Practically everybody in Australia is familiar with Ring-tailed and Silver-Grey Possums, those nocturnal, pop-eyed ragamuffins given to inimitable, though not always popular, habits of roof-bouncing and rose-pruning in the small hours when the world is their own, or at least so they think!

Not so widely known, however, are the more specialised possums: ...'

Fleay 1947, p 1

WHAT IS A POSSUM?

Ask anyone to name an Australian marsupial and they will probably think of a kangaroo or the Koala first. And yet the very first mainland Australian mammal to be recognised as a marsupial by the early European explorers was a possum. In 1770, James Cook and Joseph Banks saw a large kangaroo at the Endeavour River near the Barrier Reef and were amazed by these hopping animals, but because their specimen was an immature female, they did not notice any pouch nor realise it was a marsupial. But they did record an animal that they knew belonged to the 'opossum tribe' because it was a female with two young in the pouch. Prior to this, the only record of an Australian marsupial was of a Tammar Wallaby observed by a shipwrecked Dutch merchant on the Houtman Abrolhos off the coast of Western Australia.

If we do happen to think about possums we are most likely to curse them because of their anti-social behaviour in urban areas where they keep people awake at night cavorting on the rooftops. They also leave reminders of their activities such as urine stains on the ceiling or a destroyed rose bed or almond tree. Campers deep in the Australian bush may talk of being terrorised by marauding possums raiding tents for food in the dead of night. In New Zealand millions of possums are killed each year as the authorities try to control this introduced pest. Such is the general perception of possums. Unfortunately this is a rather biased view about one species, the Common Brushtail Possum. As a child, I lived at the edge of a small town on the banks of the local creek. Then, the brushtail possums who dared to come up from the creek and attack our garden risked being shot. I now wonder if there are any left along my creek because their numbers have declined greatly in Australian forests and woodlands.

The Common Brushtail Possum is not the only species of possum. There are 13 species of large Australian possums belonging to two families: the Phalangeridae with five species and the Pseudocheiridae with eight. The most common, widely distributed and best understood of these are the Common Brushtail Possum (*Trichosurus vulpecula*), Mountain Brushtail Possum (*T. caninus*), Common Ringtail Possum (*Pseudocheirus peregrinus*) and the Greater Glider (*Petauroides volans*). These and the Western Ringtail Possum (*Pseudocheirus occidentalis*) are the focus of this book but some information about other species is also included.

These possums are all arboreal herbivores (tree-dwelling plant eaters) and although they have been known to science for a long time, our understanding of their biology has only grown quite recently. Ecological thinking about marsupials in Australia was dominated by kangaroos until the late 1970s and research on forest-dwelling marsupials only began in earnest after the growth of public interest in forest conservation at about that time. Most of this research has focused on the Common Brushtail Possum with more than 1000 scientific papers having been published, the majority concentrating on its anatomy, physiology, and pest status in New Zealand. In the last twenty years there has been much more ecological research on these species in response to the impacts of continued habitat destruction on arboreal marsupials.

What's in a name?

The first marsupial recorded by Europeans was the Brazilian Opossum *Didelphis marsupialis*, observed by Spanish explorers of the New World in 1500. It was a female 'bearing her whelps about with her in an outward belly much like unto a great bag or purse'. At the time of Cook and Banks' voyage in 1770 there was still almost nothing known of the biology of these strange animals, so when they saw that arboreal marsupial in Queensland, they immediately likened it to the Brazilian Opossum. And the name stuck. The problem is that the Opossums of North and South America are representatives of the carnivorous marsupials (polyprotodonts) rather than the herbivorous diprotodont line of these Australian marsupials. This is one of the fundamental divisions in the taxonomy of marsupials and the use of the same common name has caused considerable confusion over the years.

For many years the 'O' had been dropped in the vernacular Australian usage but it took some time for the scientific societies and literature to catch up, especially in New Zealand. Even in 1777 James Burney, reporting on travels with James Cook, mentions finding a 'posswon' in Tasmania. Until 1980 many common names — for example Vulpine Phalanger, Brush-tailed Opossum, Australian Opossum, Australian Phalanger as well as 'possum' — were used. At that time the Australian Mammal Society adopted a list of recommended common names and formally removed the 'O' from the name of the Australian arboreal herbivores. This was also adopted in 1981 in New Zealand.

Even the term 'playing possum' comes from a behavioural characteristic of the American Virginia Opossum (*Didelphis virginiana*). When confronted by a predator and unable to escape, the opossum turns to attack, hissing and growling. If caught and shaken, the opossum suddenly goes limp, rolling over with eyes shut and tongue lolling as if dead. If the predator then loses interest, the opossum quickly recovers and runs off. Australian possums do not behave in this way, so perhaps we should call it 'playing opossum'!

THE FAMILIES OF LARGE POSSUMS

There are six families of possums. The Phalangeridae includes the brushtail possums, the Scaly-tailed Possum and the cuscuses. The Pseudocheiridae contains the ringtail possums and the Greater Glider. There are also four families of small possums and gliders: the pygmy possums (Burramyidae), the Honey Possum (Tarsipedidae), the Feathertail Glider (Acrobatidae) and the small gliding possums (Petauridae). The relationship between these possum families is illustrated in Figure 1.1.

Brushtail possums and cuscuses — Phalangeridae

The first Australasian marsupial discovered by Europeans was a phalangerid. In the mid 16th Century the Portuguese governor of the Moluccas described an animal from that region called 'kuskus' by the locals, a name still in use today. This species was undoubtedly *Phalanger orientalis* the Grey or Northern Common Cuscus but its discovery was unheralded for over two centuries until it was again discovered by science and described in 1766. There is also some confusion surrounding the 'Opossum' reported by Joseph Banks at the Endeavour River near present-day Cooktown in Queensland. It was first thought to be a ringtail but only brushtails are found within a 200-kilometre radius of Cooktown. This possum was not eaten when caught in 1770, unlike the first kangaroo, but the specimen cannot be unequivocally located and identified to solve this riddle.

There are 19 species divided into six genera. *Trichosurus* (brushtail

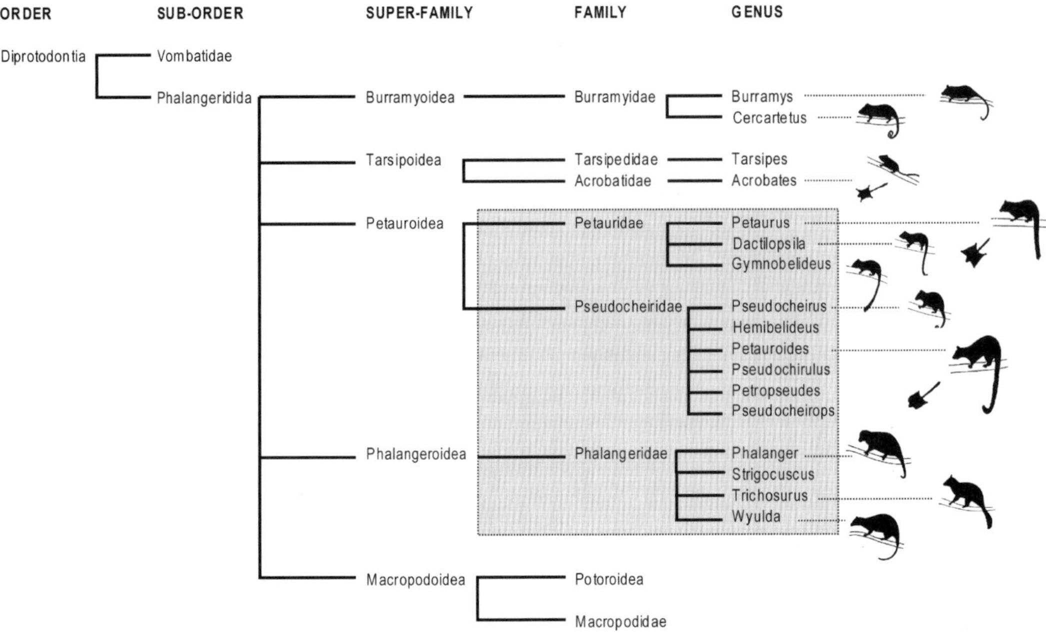

Figure 1.1 This family tree shows the relationships of the possum families within the Diprotodontia. The shaded area contains the genera included in this book and shows their close relationship to the small gliders.

possums) and *Wyulda* (Scaly-tailed Possum) are found only in Australia and the others — *Phalanger, Spilocuscus, Strigocuscus* and *Ailurops* — are types of cuscus found from northern Australia through New Guinea to the eastern half of the Indonesian archipelago and Melanesia. The discovery, relationships, description, distribution and abundance of all the Australian species are discussed in Chapter 4.

The Phalangeridae range in size from about one to four and a half kilograms and generally have a solid, rotund appearance. They are excellent climbers with a powerful grip, usually moving slowly and deliberately. This is greatly assisted by the opposable 'thumb' on the hind feet. Cuscuses all have the first two digits of the fore feet opposable to the other three. They all use their front paws to manipulate leaves or fruit into the mouth but not to pick them off a branch or the ground. The face is generally short, the nose is naked and moist and the protruding eyes are directed forward. The ears which are naked on the inner surface, are variable in length, being quite long on Common Brushtail Possums when compared with the Common Spotted Cuscus which has short, rounded ears almost buried in the fur (Figure 1.2).

The coat is soft with a dense underfur and can be extremely variable in colour, within and between species. The Common Brushtail Possum can vary from grey to red to black and the male Common Spotted Cuscus is spotted reddish grey and white, while the female is usually plain grey on

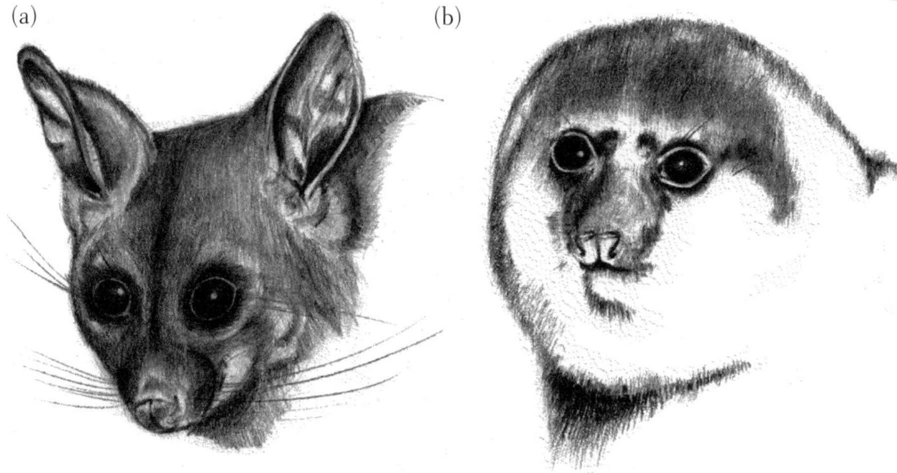

Figure 1.2 Variation in head shape, paws and tails of the Phalangeridae. (a) Common Brushtail Possum (b) Common Spotted Cuscus (c) Scaly-tailed Possum

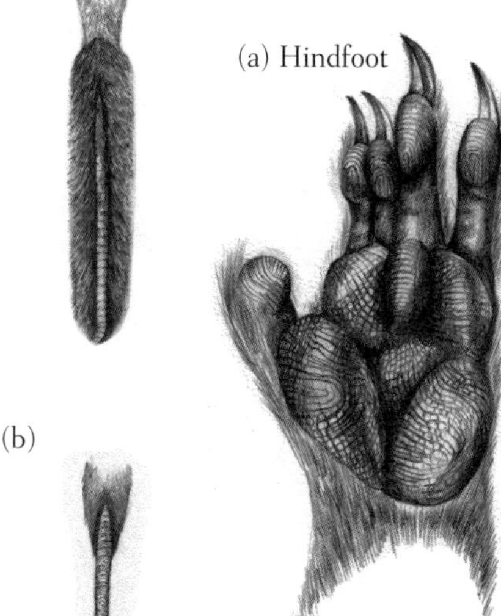

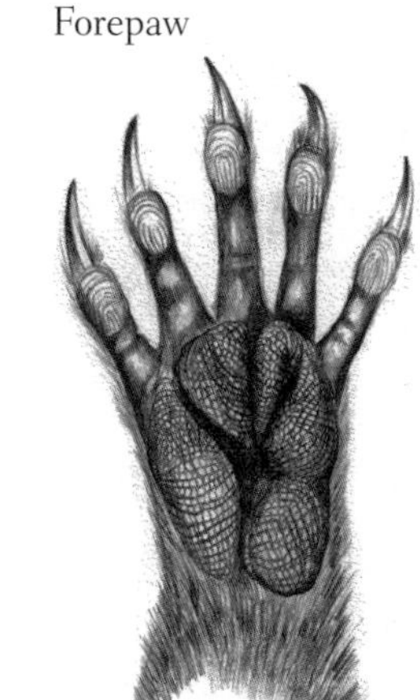

the back. There is also considerable variation in the relatively long tail of the Phalangeridae — from the brushtail possums which have a well furred tail except for a naked granulated strip along most of the undersurface and which is not strongly prehensile (grasping), to the almost naked and strongly prehensile tail of the Scaly-tailed Possum and cuscus tails which range between these two extremes but are always strongly prehensile.

Ringtail possums — Pseudocheiridae

This family contains the ringtail possums and the Greater Glider. They are more closely related to the little gliders (Family Petauridae) than to the Phalangeridae but are sufficiently distinct to be placed in their own family. A Common Ringtail Possum collected from the Sydney region on Cook's 1770 voyage was the first to be described and was initially named *Didelphis peregrinus* by Boddaert in 1785. The second specimen was also collected during one of James Cook's voyages, this time from Adventure Bay in Tasmania in 1777, but this individual appears to have been illustrated only, rather than preserved. Ringtail possums are found in Australia and New Guinea and on a few very close islands. All six genera of pseudocheirids are found in Australia, represented by eight species. Another nine species occur in the islands to the north.

These intermediate sized possums range from about 150 grams (the New Guinean species *Pseudochirulus mayeri*) to two kilograms, but most are around one kilogram. They are all extremely agile, making great use of their fifth appendage, the prehensile tail. The tail is long and mostly tapered, except in the Greater Glider, the only gliding member of this family, which uses its long tail as a rudder when gliding rather than for grasping. The opposable thumb on the hind feet aids their agility, and the first two toes on the front foot, which are opposable to the other three, enable them to grip small branches. Except in the Greater Glider, the ears are small, rounded and furred on the outside and the fur tends to be short and fine (Figure 1.3).

Figure 1.3 Variation in head shape, paws and tails of the Pseudocheiridae (a) Common Ringtail Possum (b) Greater Glider

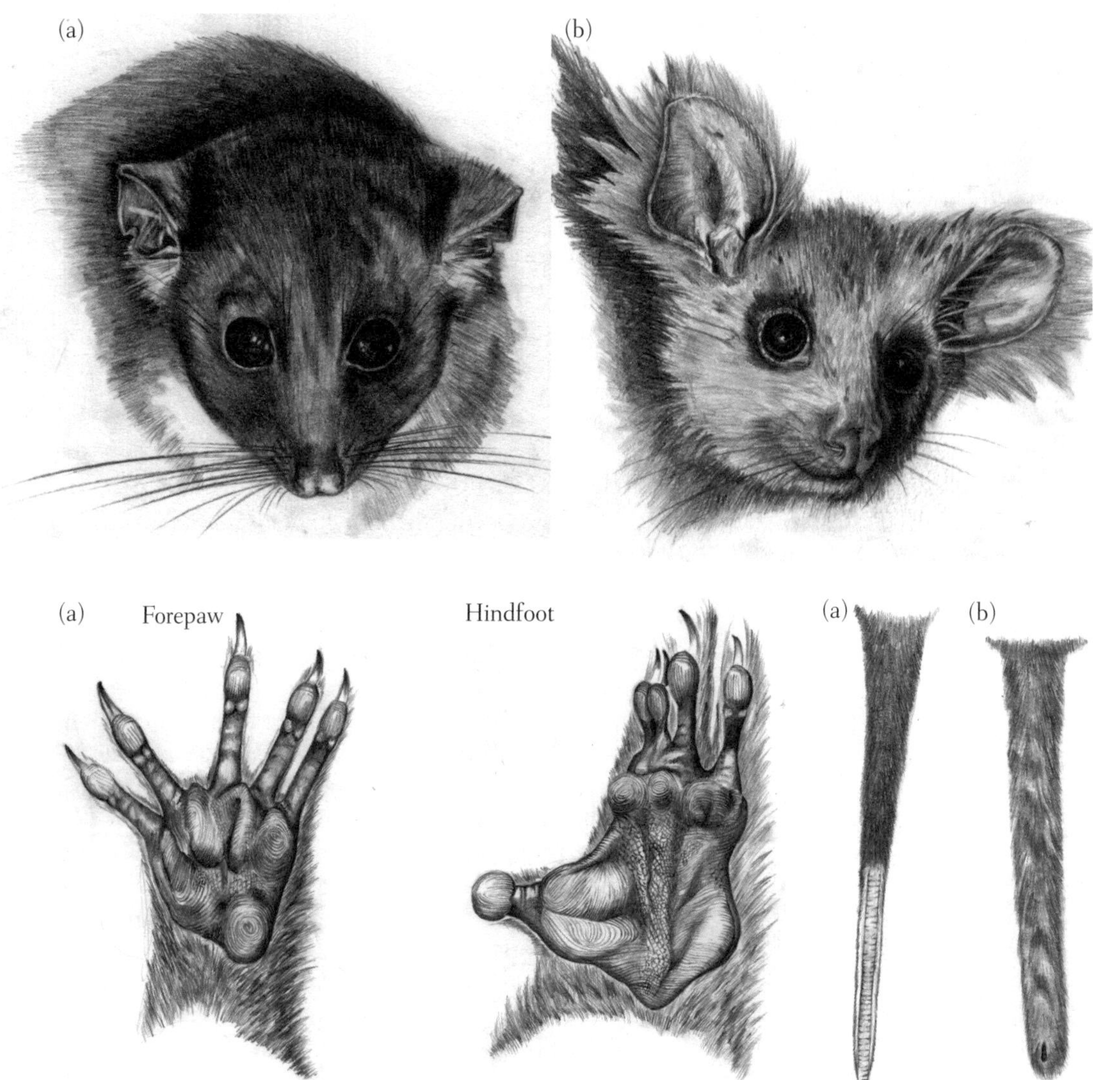

POSSUMS AND PEOPLE

Possums have always been an integral part of Australian folklore. They were a significant resource for the Aboriginal people and some of the early European settlers. The large numbers of brushtail possums in some areas meant that people were familiar with them, and often a person was nicknamed 'Possum'. Take, for example, the story of *The Man Called Possum*. He was a gentle, animal loving 'bush recluse' who lived along the Murray River in the Renmark area of South Australia. His name was Jim, he called himself 'Nifty', but the people who knew him called him 'Possum' because they often saw him climbing trees to get honey and because he always hid from people. It was an affectionate nickname.

POSSUMS AND THE ABORIGINAL PEOPLE

Possums are an extremely important part of the interwoven spiritual and physical lives of the Aboriginal people. For these people, the land and all its inhabitants were created by ancestral beings who had human qualities of courage, love, friendship, anger and hatred. The possum spirit in central Australia, for example, is extremely curious and often mischievous, but is also kind and very active. Sometimes the spirits became part of the landscape. Such places became sacred to Aborigines and can be seen only by initiated men. Kata Tjuta (the Olgas) in Uluru National Park is one such place associated with possum dreamings where only the initiated men know the stories. The laws for looking after the land, established by those ancestral beings, are the basis for the Aboriginal custodianship of the land, which ensures that their needs for food and shelter will continue to be met.

The dreaming stories of the spirit ancestors of central Australia criss-cross the landscape and include many sites and stories relating to the possum ancestors. In one story, an old Possum Man called Upambura (also known as 'Lover Man') travels to Uluru to find a young woman and take her back to his own country near Napperby (north-east of Alice Springs). On his way back, Possum Man and his Pitjantjatjara wife emerge from the ground near Haasts Bluff to find the Rainbow Serpents, who had been travelling from the north creating soaks and watercourses, making a large home for themselves under a rock. Possum Man is furious because this is his country and he sends them away, back to Lajamanu to the north where they came from. Possum Man and his wife then returned to their home.

This and other stories are told by Clifford Possum Tjapaltjarri, an Anmatyerre man from central Australia and a famous Aboriginal artist. When telling this story Clifford Possum bursts into laughter and in many of his paintings he depicts the possum ancestors as a 'lover boy' with allusions to the presence of enlarged sexual organs generally resulting from too much ancestral philandering!

Another story is of a confrontation between the Rock Wallaby Men from Port Augusta and the northern Possum Men. The Possum Men were conducting important ceremonies when the Rock Wallabies burst in and a fight broke out. Eventually the two sides called an end to the fighting and agreed to exchange the important ceremonial knowledge. They established a big corroboree camp and the surrounding area was known as good possum country before the arrival of white settlers. In fact Aboriginal law completely protects some important sites such as these from hunting, even during droughts, in order to ensure the survival of their food species. Unfortunately possums have now almost completely disappeared from this region although they are still very important in the dreaming songs and rituals performed today.

The great importance of possum in the diet of Aboriginal people was recognised in early writings from the new colony. Unlike the coastal people, who relied mostly on seafood, the people between Parramatta and the Blue Mountains (the 'inland' people) depended more on small animals and plants. Indeed, writing in 1802, Ensign Francis Barrallier considered that possum was the most important source of protein for these people and suggested that kangaroo was caught less readily and eaten less frequently.

These inland people were described as 'climbers of trees and men who lived by hunting' who would 'ascend the tallest trees after the opossum and flying squirrel' (Plate 1). Methods of catching possums varied, probably depending on the country and type of possum. An 1813 painting (Plate 2) illustrates a method used by the 'inland' Aborigines to hunt possums.

Smoke from a fire lit in the base of a hollow tree forces the possums from their hollows; a hunter then knocks them to the ground.

The stone tool technology of the area supported the importance of possums and other tree-dwelling animals in the Aboriginal diets. The edge-ground hatchet, used to enlarge the base hollows and cut toeholds in the trees, was one of their most common tools. Early accounts also mention the use of traps and snares for catching possums. These would have been most useful for the Common Brushtail, which spends more time on the ground than other species.

In 1863 John Gould described in detail the importance of possums in the Aboriginal diet:

> This animal constitutes a considerable part of the food of the natives, who diligently search for it, and having discovered a tree in which it is secreted, ascend it with surprising agility; the position of the animal being ascertained, a hole is cut with their little axes sufficiently large to admit the naked arm; it is then seized by the tail, the chopping and jarring of the tree not inducing it to leave its retreat, and before it has time to bite, or use its powerful claws, it is deprived of life by a blow against the side of the tree, and thrown to the ground; its captor proceeding to his encampment with a dinner in perspective. I have frequently eaten its flesh myself, and found it far from disagreeable. (From Gould's account of '*Phalangista (Trichosurus) vulpecula*'.)

In arid and semi-arid Australia possums were common in many areas and were an important Aboriginal food source. Aborigines hunted the possums when they became active on moonlit nights or cut them from their tree holes. In the Flinders Ranges of South Australia possums were a primary food for the Adnyamathanha people, who would sing a special possum-hunting song before the hunt. In this area the people recall seeing fifty or sixty possums in a single tree. These recollections reinforce the fact that possums were both plentiful and important in this area. While Gould recorded that 'the natives' caught possums by the tail, the Flinders Ranges people suggest that the hunter had to catch hold of the head and wring it because it was impossible to pull them out by the tail.

The way of eating possum is described by Margaret-Mary Turner, a respected Arrernte woman from Alice Springs in her book *Arrernte Foods*:

> You gut them, close them up with a wooden skewer, singe the fur off and then cook them in hot soil. When you eat them after they have been eating nectar from bloodwood trees, they taste really sweet, especially the milk guts. (p 45)

The meat is reportedly quite juicy rather than being dry like rabbit and some Aboriginal people have commented that the gut and intestines can be eaten raw because it is 'already cooked', perhaps an effect of oils from the eucalypt leaves in the diet of the possum. Gould described the meat as 'white and delicate, and not unlike that of a rabbit.'

Because of its wide distribution and abundance, the Common Brushtail Possum was the most commonly eaten species, but Aboriginal people also ate other possum species. John Gould described the Common Ringtail Possum flesh as being 'delicate, juicy and well tasted, and is much prized by the Aborigines'. There are also records of Aboriginal people hunting the Herbert River Ringtail Possum in north Queensland. They searched for them in fern clumps by climbing trees with the aid of a climbing cane. The Greater Glider was another popular species. Gould records that hunters located gliders by detecting hairs caught on the bark around tree hollows or from scratches in the bark; the hunters then cut them out as they did for the brushtail possum. Scaly-tailed Possums and cuscuses were also hunted for food.

Possums were important to Aborigines not only for food — they also provided other resources such as clothing and string. The early European settlers observed that Aborigines living only a small distance inland differed from coastal people in several ways, not the least being that they made cloaks from possum and kangaroo fur. Inland people also made 'lines' (string) from possum fur as well as from the bark of Kurrajong and Stringybark trees. In the Kimberley region, the fur of the Scaly-tailed Possum was spun into string. An especially unusual artefact collected by a Lutheran missionary at Hermannsburg in central Australia in about 1910 is a possum tooth engraver used for engraving designs on wooden objects such as boomerangs.

The skin of the brushtail possum was particularly important for making mantles and sleeping rugs. Its value varied with the region. Tasmanian skins were generally preferred after the arrival of Europeans in Australia and Gould believed that a Tasmanian possum sleeping rug was worth three times one from the mainland because of the greater density (and therefore warmth) of the fur. Skins were made into blankets throughout Australia including the deserts, where the winter nights can be extremely cold. They could be used as a blanket, a cloak (pinned at the neck by a bone pin), or as a cloth for catching food (insects and fruit) shaken from trees. The skin was removed before the animal was cooked, and then softened by rubbing and scraping with small, flat, sharp pieces of stone. The skins were then sewn together using an awl made from kangaroo bone and spunfur string, or sinews prepared from the tail.

Spun possum fur had a variety of uses: practical, ceremonial and decorative. The pubic tassel worn by men was made of strings attached to a woven band. Human hair was generally preferred but possum fur was also used. In Arnhem Land, finely spun possum fur was highly valued, especially for ceremonial objects. In its non-ceremonial form, spun possum fur was used without restriction including armlets and aprons for the women. Elsewhere, string bags and nets were made of spun fur or sinew. In 1807 George Barrington recorded that young Aboriginal women in New South Wales wore a little apron made from possum or kangaroo skin, cut into slips and hung from the waist. Apparently these were worn only until the girls were 'taken by men'.

The various cuscus species have been very important to the people in the islands to the north for food, clothing and decoration. Some, such as the Selayar Moslems or Sulawesi Christians, will not eat cuscus though they may keep them as pets, or for social status, or may trade them for their meat or fur. Indeed it would seem that the present distribution of cuscuses has been greatly influenced by trade between the islands. For example, the Northern Common Cuscus was introduced to New Ireland prehistorically; the isolated population of Common Spotted Cuscus on Selayar Island was probably introduced in pre-Moslem times by seafaring people for food, and the same species appears to have been introduced to New Ireland just before World War II.

THE LAST 200 YEARS

The Common Brushtail Possum was widely distributed and abundant across Australia when the First Fleet arrived. Now, as a result of the impact of the European settlement of the continent, it has all but disappeared from more than half of its previous range and is common only in Tasmania, Kangaroo Island and some of our cities. The direct impact of the colonists began early. In 1889 Carl Lumholtz described the young colonists as 'very zealous possum hunters' who hunted for sport on moonlit nights. And of course, the first requirement for the new settlement was to clear the land, removing the habitat of many animal species. All possum species appear to have declined in distribution and abundance over the last 200 years, although the information available for other species is much more limited than it is for the Brushtail.

Just how common the Common Brushtail Possum once was can be gleaned from many personal accounts, diaries, journals and records of explorers, settlers and government agencies. Remains of small mammals in cave deposits are another indicator of the species present just prior to the arrival of Europeans, especially in the arid zone. Analysis of such deposits has demonstrated that brushtail possums were present right through the arid two-thirds of Australia and were not restricted to the major watercourses as they largely are now.

Early explorers often mentioned possums, having observed them directly or noting them as Aboriginal food. In inland NSW, they were apparently not common when Charles Sturt passed through but accounts from central Australia suggest they were quite common there, especially in 1894 and 1932–35. More recently the poet Keith Garvey wrote of finding a possum in every hollow spout of the River Red Gums along the rivers, especially the Murray–Darling system and in the drier ridge country; where the trees had been ring-barked, he observed heaps of possum dung remaining in the stumps and logs. These observations were made prior to the introduction of myxomatosis to eradicate rabbits and Garvey believed it also killed the possums.

In southern central Queensland, near St George, the Munro family purchased a property in 1881. In his diaries (as published by Fairbairn

1983), William Ross Munro graphically describes possum populations in that area:

> The possums which were there in numbers when the place was purchased during '81, increased to an alarming extent. They were there in millions. At night, on any night, they could be seen in clusters like fruit on a laden tree. Most of them lived in the hollows of gum trees along the 15-mile river frontage. All along that frontage, and for 2 or 3 miles out from it, the coolibahs were thick.
>
> The general opinion is that possums live on gum leaves. Gum leaves were thick on all the trees, with no evidence of cropping; but the coolibahs were denuded, just stark skeletons without leaves. Also, those possums reduced the grasses to an extent which cannot be accurately estimated. Did a fall of rain bring a green shoot on the broken plains in the timbered country, and although no other stock were in that paddock, those possums would keep the shoot level with the earth.
>
> A couple of indications are given as to their numbers. Their pads on the ground were so thick that one would think a man had been dragging a bullock chain aimlessly. On favoured areas, and particularly on the frontages, it mattered not what stock were running that paddock; in the morning there would not be a track of a sheep, a horse or a bullock — the possums would have obliterated them with their own tracks during the night. And they kept on increasing in numbers — increasing and increasing! In addition to what they ate they befouled much grass, making it unpalatable to the sheep. They were indeed a curse.
>
> Then Nature played another of her jokes: she sent 469 points of rain in May, to be followed by 124 in June. The country did respond to that. The winter herbages flourished; the land was green with wild carrots; the stock revelled in that choice pasture and all was well with them.
>
> But there was one tragedy among the livestock — perhaps 'native fauna' is a better term. Those millions and millions of possums just were not there after the flood. No man saw them die. No one knows what afflicted them. Doubtless every hollow tree served as a vault in which the crumbling bones of possums may be found to this day. Those countless myriads of possums just ceased to be. They were regarded as a pest, almost a curse, and overnight, as it were, they were wiped out by some mysterious influence which has never been solved.
>
> As an indication of how complete was the eradication, it can be mentioned that Roy, my eldest son, born in '86 asked me during '96 to explain what a possum was like. He had never seen one.
>
> The possums came back gradually.

Dramatic descriptions such as these demonstrate huge fluctuations in possum numbers in some areas but the causes are difficult to determine. The impact of the Australian fur industry on possum populations is also hard to assess but in some areas it probably led to population decline. In 1923 Frederick Wood Jones in South Australia wrote of the need to protect possums because of the destructiveness of the fur trade. Possum fur was considered to be a valuable resource soon after Sydney was first established, as was the fur of the Greater Glider. The Common Brushtail

Possum was found to have dense and soft fur that adheres to its skin after death, making the pelt suitable for tanning. A thriving trade was developed and brushtail skins were sold as 'Skunk' when shorn and dyed, 'Beaver' and 'Adelaide Chinchilla', as well as 'Opossum'! The Greater Glider was spared from the impact of the fur trade because the skin could not be tanned satisfactorily, but ringtail skins were sought although fewer were taken.

In general the furriers preferred the thicker, woollier possum skins from the cooler areas, especially Tasmania. The 'Tasmanian Blacks' and 'Monaro Blues' were particularly desirable. The skin of continental ringtails was too thin to be highly valuable and ringtails from Tasmania were considered to be of better quality. The total number of possum skins sold from Australia is not known, but to gain some idea, more than four million pelts were sold in London and New York in 1906; over 100,000 possums were killed in South Australia during a four month period in 1920, and in the 1920s between two and three million pelts were marketed annually. Most of the ringtail skins originated in Tasmania with some 7.5 million being taken between 1923 and 1955. In Victoria in 1959 only 2500 ringtails were taken compared with a harvest of 107 000 brushtails. The possum fur trade is now a limited one restricted to Tasmania.

The fact that throughout most of its range the Common Brushtail Possum has disappeared or is rare is frequently clouded by its often-annoying abundance in the cities and its devastating presence in New Zealand. There it has readily colonised the native Podocarp, Rata and mixed hardwood forests in both the North and South Islands and become a mixed blessing. On one hand it has provided a substantial income to the fur industry but as a carrier of bovine tuberculosis it has cost the agricultural industry greatly and has proven to be an environmental vandal. The extremely dense populations in many areas, and their preference for particular plant species, have resulted in severe damage to these forests and to some of the indigenous berry-eating bird species. Indeed it is considered to be the worst introduced pest — much more so than the rabbit, which has been bad enough.

Acclimatisation societies imported and liberated brushtail possums into New Zealand from 1837 to 1959, primarily for the establishment of a fur industry. The majority of the stock was Tasmanian (because of their more commercially valuable pelt) but some also came from mainland Australia. Overall there was a preference for the 'Tasmanian Black', which was keenly sought by trappers and the fur industry in general. Imports from Australia occurred intermittently until 1930 and the whole process was advocated and supported by government, pressured by the acclimatisation societies. A typical annual report from one of these societies stated 'We shall be doing a great service to the country in stocking these large areas (of rough bush hills) with this valuable and harmless animal', demonstrating the attitude at the time. Later importations were sought to 'improve' the breed but this was achieved by the liberation of New Zealand bred possums into new areas and this continued until 1957. The peak of introductions and liberations was from 1890 to 1930. By 1923, some New Zealanders were beginning to question the wisdom of the introduction, noting the destruction of the berry-bearing forest trees.

The New Zealand possum population is widely distributed and estimated at about 70 million. Some 1.5 million skins are exported each year but this trade has little impact on the populations. Despite the annual value of the fur trade — about $20 million — considerable effort and expense is now being directed towards the control of the species with an annual cost of at least NZ$60 million — $20 million in research and $40 million in animal destruction. This does not include the cost of disease control and lost productivity for the livestock industries. Eradication is probably impossible but control is essential given the agricultural and environmental costs to the country.

CHAPTER 3

EVOLUTION, FORM AND FUNCTION

Fundamental to the survival of a species are its body size and shape; its energy needs; its ability to sense and react to the environment, to reproduce and to respond to other animals of the same and different species; and its ability to survive difficulties present in the environment. In many ways the basic body shape, internal structures and functioning of possums differ little from the general marsupial plan. Other attributes are highly evolved and specialised to meet the specific challenges of their arboreal, browsing, herbivorous lifestyle. Here we trace the origin of the Australian species of large possums, their relationships and their characteristic body form and locomotion, before considering their energy needs and senses. Most of the research into the anatomy and physiology of possums has been carried out for the Common Brushtail Possum.

THE EVOLUTION AND RELATIONSHIPS OF POSSUMS

Australian land mammals can be divided into three broad groups: monotremes (Platypus and Echidna), marsupials, and placentals (bats, rats and mice and introduced species). Marsupials, which include possums, have been the dominant group. About two-thirds of the world's marsupial species are found in Australia where they have evolved to fill the available habitats, while the placental species (which are more common in the northern hemisphere) appear to have arrived here much later and represent only about four per cent of all placental species. For a long time marsupials have been considered 'inferior' to placental mammals. Even in 1987 the Youth News of the Mammal Society of England still defined a marsupial as '...a primitive mammal distinguished by young being born in an immature condition and continuing its development in its mothers abdominal pouch'. In fact they differ, not by being more primitive, but by having a differently evolved reproductive system in which the kidney (urinary) and sex (genital) ducts are in different positions relative to each other.

The oldest marsupial fossils have been found in North America and are thought to be 100 million years old. Some species moved to South America where they successfully evolved and then radiated through Antarctica to Australasia when these continents were part of the same landmass, Gondwana. The subsequent long period of separation of the landmasses has resulted in the evolutionary distinction of the two primary groups of marsupials, which are now only distantly related: the ameridelphians (from the Americas) and the australidelphians (from Australasia). The opossums of America and possums of Australasia are therefore only very distantly connected marsupials.

At the beginning of the tertiary period (65 million years before the present — MYBP), Gondwana was located somewhere near the South Pole. The climate was warm and moist — not frozen as Antarctica is now — and much of the Australian portion was covered with broad-leaved rainforest. But Gondwana was breaking up. The Australian landmass was drifting north and its links with Antarctica were severed somewhere between 46 and 35 million years ago. As the continent drifted northwards, it began to cool and dry out, the rainforests decreased and eucalypt forests, banksias, casuarinas and grasslands flourished (Figure 3.1).

Three groups of species evolved within the Australidelphia: carnivorous marsupials (Dasyuromorphia), bandicoots and bilbies (Peramelemorphia) and the more specialised herbivorous marsupials (Diprotodontia). As indicated in Figure 1.1, the diprotodonts include the wombats and Koala (Vombatidae) and the Phalangeridida (possums, pygmy possums, gliders, honey possum and all the kangaroos, wallabies and potoroos). The name Diprotodontia comes from the presence of a single pair of long, strong, pointed incisors (biting teeth) in the bottom jaw of all these species — it literally means 'two front teeth'. These lower incisors are almost horizontal and are separated from the teeth behind by a large gap. Another characteristic common to all the diprotodonts is called *syndactyly*, in which the first and second toes are joined together, appearing to be a single toe with two claws.

The oldest known possum-like fossils have been found in deposits in the Lake Eyre and Lake Frome basins of arid northern South Australia. These deposits have been dated at 26.0–23.3 million years old and contain many primitive types of marsupials. At the time these central Australian fossil beds were deposited, the country was covered by

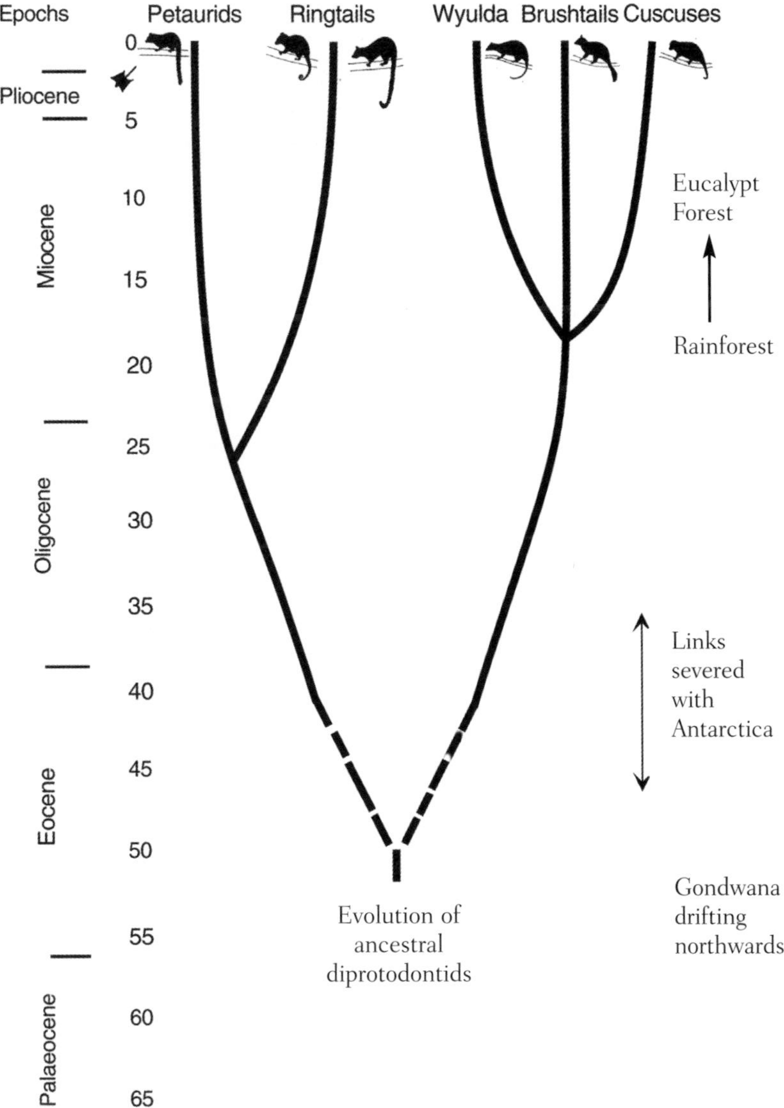

Figure 3.1 Possible sequence of events during the evolution of the phalangerids, pseudocheirids and petaurids. Timescale: million years before present (MYBP).

rainforests interspersed with open spaces and vast permanent wetlands supporting flamingoes, dolphins and crocodiles.

The incredibly rich fossil deposits found in the Riversleigh area of western Queensland have enabled dramatic progress to be made in unravelling the story of possum evolution. Twenty million years ago Riversleigh was covered by a lush rainforest, which supported an abundant and diverse marsupial fauna, including possums. This fossil possum fauna contains many primitive and extinct families but most of the Riversleigh remains are representatives of families still living today.

Brushtails, cuscuses and the Scaly-tailed Possum had all appeared by the early to mid Miocene (Figure 3.2) in addition to two other extinct phalangeroid families — the Miralinidae and the Ektopodontidae. The ektopodontids were quite common in the central Australian fossil deposits and were still present in the 4.5 million year old deposits at Hamilton in Victoria, but the miralinids were not common in the Oligo–Miocene deposits and appear to have become extinct sometime during the Miocene.

Figure 3.2 Skull (a) and lower jaw (b) of the Riversleigh Brushtail Possum *Trichosurus dicksoni*. These Miocene brushtails have many similarities with the living species. (c) Lower jaw of the Cuscus *Strigocuscus reidi* found at Riversleigh. The third premolar is very large indicating a varied diet. (Drawn from Vickers-Rich and Rich 1993).

A great variety of ringtails have been found in the Riversleigh fossils with more species present in the late Oligocene and early Miocene than there are now. Most of the early species are quite unusual and primitive with no living descendants. Of the ringtail possums that still exist, *Pseudocheirops* is the oldest genus with at least three species found in Oligo–Miocene deposits, the oldest of which is the Rock Ringtail Possum which has been found in 5 million-year-old deposits at Riversleigh. There were also representatives of the 'megafauna' with an enormous ringtail, a *Pseudokoala*, having being found. Three species of these large arboreal possums have been described with one estimated as being nine or ten kilograms. These large possums were present in late Miocene to early Pleistocene deposits (10 to 1 MYBP).

Like the majority of the Australian fauna, possums originated in the ancient rainforests and then were confronted by the need to survive in a drier environment with different plant species. There were apparently three responses to this challenge: some like the ektopodontids became extinct; others, like many of the ringtails, retreated with the rainforest into north-east Queensland and New Guinea, and the brushtails adapted to the new conditions. Riversleigh is now part of the wet–dry tropics of northern Australia. In the dry season it is an inhospitable dusty eucalypt woodland that becomes transformed in the wet with lush grass growth and fast-flowing rivers fringed with luxuriant vegetation. Few possums are found in this area now and if they are, they are most likely to be Northern Brushtails. Around 15 million years ago, the Australia–New Guinea continental plate collided with South-east Asia and the resultant crumpling of the land mass produced the New Guinea highlands where many of the ringtail and cuscus species are now found.

The definition and description of the various species of living possums and the relationships within families and genera has changed frequently since their first discovery. The obvious variation in body form of the Common Brushtail Possum has resulted in the description of many species and sub-species throughout its scientific history. The taxonomy of the Pseudocheiridae has been comparatively conservative until recently with their inclusion in the Petauridae and with only a few genera having been described. The ringtail possums and small gliders appear to have separated from each other about 25–30 million years ago.

Chromosomes, the thread shaped structures contained within the nucleus of an animal's cell that carry its genetic information (DNA), vary in number between species. Analysis of the number and shape of the chromosomes has significantly helped with the definition of the living species, especially within the Ringtail Possum group. The number of chromosomes found in the Phalangeridae and Pseudocheiridae varies from 10 to 22. The Brushtail Possums, Common Ringtail Possum and Lemuroid Ringtail all have 20 chromosomes and the Greater Glider has 22. The greatest variety in number occurs within the remaining ringtail possums, especially when the New Guinean species are included. The Coppery Ringtail from the New Guinean highlands has the lowest number of 10. The chromosome number of the Scaly-tailed Possum and both Australian species of cuscus is unknown. Two New Guinean cuscus species have 14 chromosomes.

BODY FORM

The skulls of brushtails and ringtails have some distinct differences in shape and structure (Figure 3.3). The broad, stoutly built skull of the phalangers has a relatively short snout, strong cheekbones (zygomatic arch) and a large vacuity (space) at the back of the palate. There are three pairs of upper incisors, which sit over the two almost horizontal (procumbent) incisors in the lower jaw. In brushtails the upper canine is small and the third pre-molar has a long cutting edge. There are four pairs of grinding molar teeth with smooth mound-like cusps similar in shape to those of the mixed-feeding ancestral possums. The Scaly-tailed Possum and cuscuses have well developed canine teeth in the upper jaw and the third premolar is very large with a sharp cutting edge. The ringtail skull is not so robust and is characterised by a pointed muzzle and several palatal vacuities (holes in the back of the palate). In the upper jaw there are three pairs of incisors, small canine teeth, three upper premolars and four pairs of molars with sharply curved ridges on the cusps. The procumbent lower incisors are compressed and blade-like.

The most obvious specialisation in these possums is the patagium or gliding membrane of the Greater Glider. It consists of a fold of skin with two layers bound together tightly by connective tissue. The muscle fibres that run through the connective tissue retract the membrane when it is not in use and control altitude while gliding. The musculature of the Greater Glider patagium is different from that found in the smaller gliders

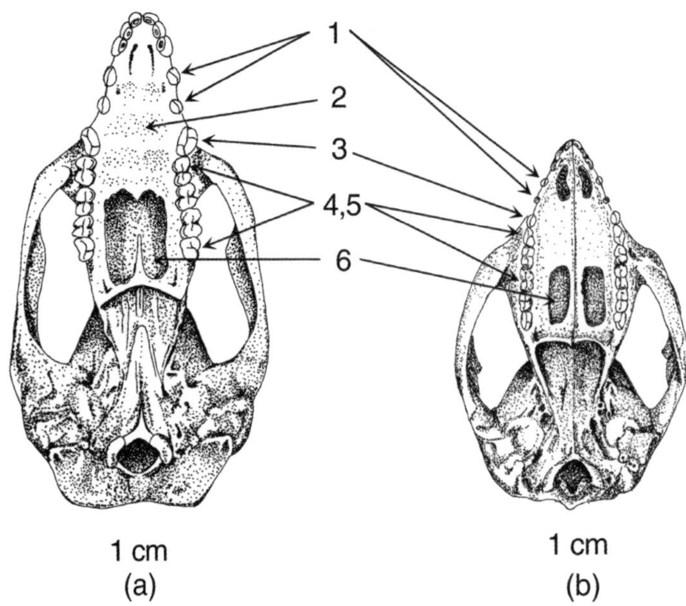

Figure 3.3
There are many features that differ between the skulls of the Common Brushtail Possum (a) and the Common Ringtail Possum (b). In addition to size and shape these include:

1. Very small canine and first premolar in ringtail.
2. Ridged palate in brushtail.
3. Large bladelike premolar curves outwards in brushtail.
4. Molar row straight and even in ringtail.
5. Crescent shaped ridges on ringtail molars, cone-like cusps on brushtail molars.
6. Two clearly separated holes in the back of the ringtail palate; brushtail palate has one hole partly divided.

(*Petaurus* species) suggesting that the ability to glide in these two groups evolved independently. The membrane on the Greater Glider extends from the elbows of the front limbs to the ankle of the hind feet and, while gliding, the hind limbs are fully extended but the forefeet are tucked under the chin with the elbows held out giving them a slightly triangular shape. In the small gliders the patagium reaches from the fifth finger of the hand to the ankle and they glide with all four legs fully extended (Figure 3.4). The Lemuroid Ringtail Possum, the species most closely related to the Greater Glider, also has a remnant gliding membrane of small flaps of skin along its flanks.

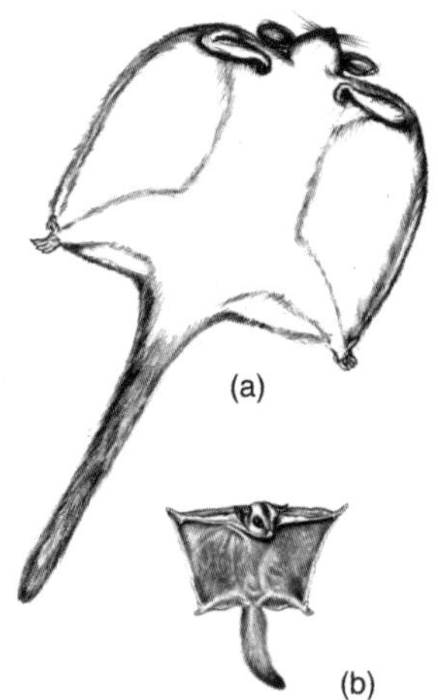

Figure 3.4
The Greater Glider (a) glides with the elbows bent while the Sugar Glider (b) has its arms fully extended.

The skeleton of the Greater Glider is also specially adapted for gliding. The long bones of the limbs are longer than in similarly sized ringtail possums and some of the vertebrae are elongated. Because of the longer vertebrae in the tail it is less flexible and no longer prehensile, making it more efficient as a rudder when gliding. The front feet of the Greater Glider are larger than other ringtails' and are armed with bigger claws, enhancing their ability to grip when landing on a tree trunk. The Lemuroid Ringtail Possum has similar but less exaggerated specialisations.

When climbing a tree trunk the front legs and then the back legs alternately grasp the trunk but on smaller branches they change to the crossed extension gait. Unlike Koalas, the possums all climb down trees head first.

Figure 3.5
How the Common Brushtail Possum moves around (from John Winter).

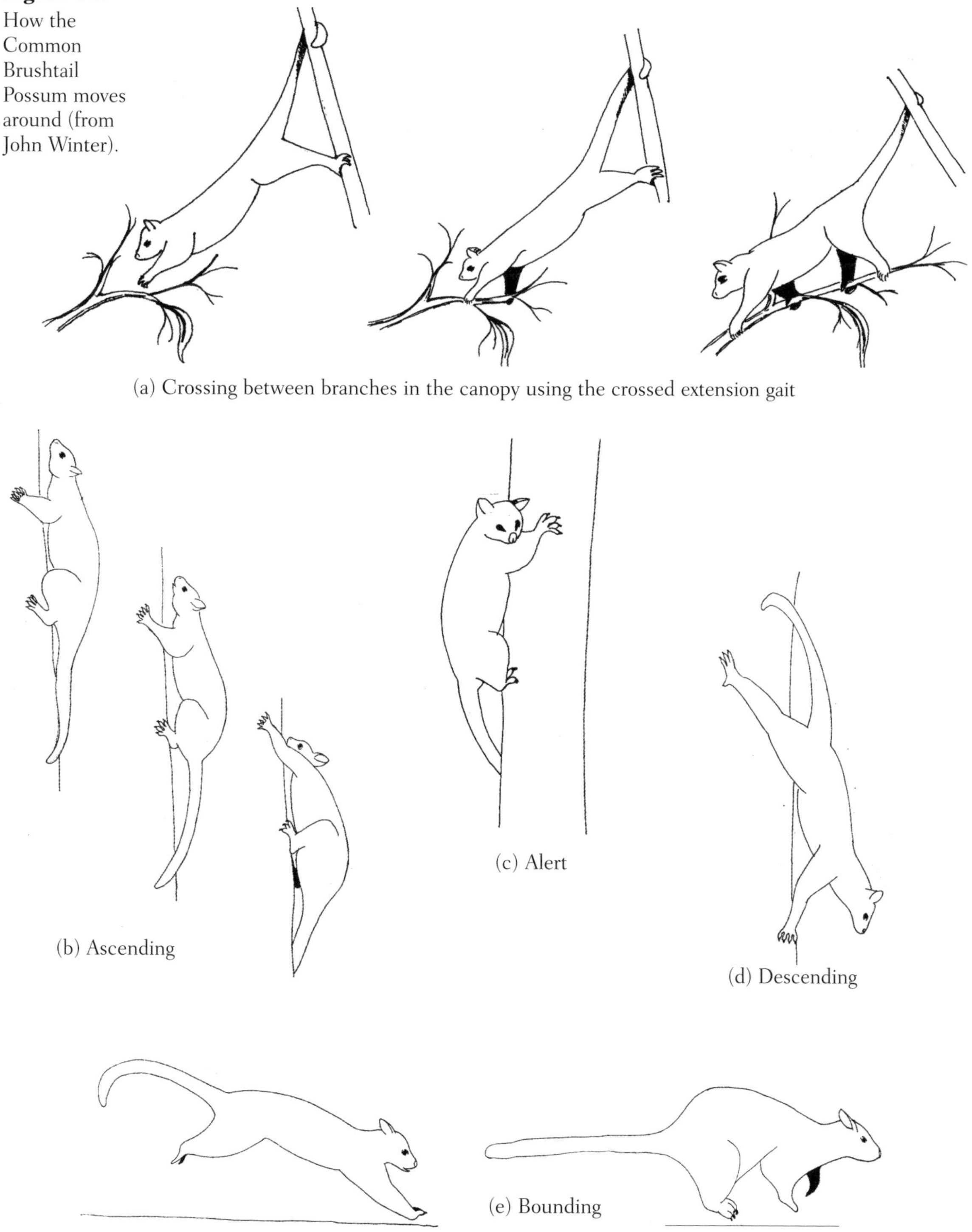

(a) Crossing between branches in the canopy using the crossed extension gait

(b) Ascending

(c) Alert

(d) Descending

(e) Bounding

When moving at low speed on flat ground most have a crossed extension walk, in which the front right leg moves with the back, left leg and vice versa. This changes to a half bound when their speed reaches 1.4 metres per second and to a bounding gait at higher speed (Figure 3.5).

ENERGETICS AND TEMPERATURE REGULATION

The daily challenge faced by all animals is to meet their metabolic requirements — the energetic costs of all the biological needs of the animal. They must obtain sufficient nutrition to survive and reproduce while also maintaining a constant body temperature. The basal metabolic rate (BMR) is a measure of the survival energy needs of an animal. Marsupials have long been known to have a lower average BMR than most placental mammals and this, in addition to lower body temperature, was one of the factors that led early researchers to believe that marsupials were 'primitive' when compared with the more familiar mammals of the time. On average, the marsupial BMR is about 70 per cent of the mean placental BMR. Both the Common Brushtail Possum and Common Spotted Cuscus have an even lower BMR of 62 per cent of the 'placental mean'. Having a lower BMR means that the animal requires less food and will survive for longer under adverse conditions.

The core body temperature of these marsupials is also lower than that for equivalent placental mammals. For the Common Brushtail Possum the core body temperature is 36.2°C and for the Common Spotted Cuscus, 34.6°C. The Brushtail can maintain a stable core body temperature up to an air temperature of 44°C but in hotter conditions they achieve stability by panting and evaporating water through the skin. The Common Spotted Cuscus also uses panting and evaporative cooling to avoid becoming overheated in hot weather and has been observed sunning itself to keep warm. Their thick, insulating fur is probably an adaptation to their preference for sleeping in the windy rainforest canopy rather than in tree hollows.

Young possums are not born with a stable body temperature and for Common Brushtail Possums the ability to maintain a constant body temperature does not develop until the young is almost old enough to leave the pouch. There is no evidence of any special mechanism to keep them warm, such as the special brown fat deposits of some placental mammals. Warmth is provided by the insulation of the pouch.

Feeding the young also increases the energy demands for females. A study by Sarah Munks of variation in energy expenditure of the Common Ringtail Possum has provided an indication of the demands of lactation. The annual energy expenditure by non-breeding adult females was 213 mega joules (MJ) and there was no significant seasonal variation. It increased to 248 MJ per annum for a female with two young but this increase was not evenly distributed throughout the year with 30 per cent of the annual energy being used during the late stages of lactation (for 24 per cent of the year). This is 30 per cent above the non-reproductive energy demands. During this late stage, breeding females use body fat accumulated during the earlier, less demanding, stages of lactation to compensate for the increased energy needs. The latter stages of lactation also coincide with the seasonal growth of young leaves, which provides the females with higher levels of energy and water in their diet.

SENSES AND THE NERVOUS SYSTEM

The brain size of possums in relation to body size is quite variable. The Greater Glider, Common Ringtail and the Southern Common Cuscus have a relatively small brain, it is an average size for the Brushtail and both the Scaly-tailed Possum and Common Spotted Cuscus appear to have a larger than expected brain size.

The Common Brushtail Possum's brain has been studied in detail and has been used as an example of a 'typical' marsupial brain for comparative studies of the structure and function of the mammalian brain. On one hand, the basic structure of the brushtail brain appears to be very old and is similar to the extinct *Wynyardia* (a wombat-like animal) that lived 15 million years ago. But far from having a typical form, it is also unusually variable in both internal and external structure. This degree of variation is uncommon in mammals. The presence of a well developed motor-somaesthetic cortex (a specific portion of the brain) correlates with the excellent manipulative skills of brushtails and provides a possible reason for the ability of these possums to survive changes in their habitat more readily than the Koala, for example, in which this part of the brain is poorly developed. The sense of smell is well developed in possums as it is in most mammals, as indicated by the presence of a prominent olfactory bulb on the brain.

The agility and accuracy of movement by possums, especially the gliders, in quite complex environments requires well-developed vision. There are some specific visual specialisations in the part of the brain associated with sight and in the structure of the eye, in which the brushtail and some other possum species differ from other mammals. The tapetum lucidum, a layer of pigment in the eye that reflects incoming light, is well developed in the possums. It is thought that this layer increases the ability of a nocturnal animal to see by reflecting light back onto the rod-shaped receptors in the retina (the back of the eye) that are specialised for detecting low levels of light. The brightness of the eyeshine when spotlighting an animal is some indication of the variation in the development of this layer — the brushtail, Greater Glider and Lemuroid Ringtail all have a very bright eyeshine.

4

CHAPTER

THE SPECIES OF LARGE AUSTRALIAN POSSUMS

PHALANGERIDAE

The brushtails (*Trichosurus* species)

The common name of these possums highlights the feature that distinguishes them most clearly from all other possums — the thick bushy tail. When translated the Latin name *Trichosurus* simply means 'hairy tail'. Their pointed snout and long ears are also distinctive as is the broad, stout skull. The genus name *Trichosurus* was introduced in 1828 by Lesson after they were called *Didelphis* in 1792 as were all other marsupials at the time, then *Ursus*, based on the common name 'New Holland Bear' and *Phalangista*. There are now two species of *Trichosurus* but from the time of their discovery there has been considerable confusion with several species having been described on the basis of variation in colour, size and furriness.

Common Brushtail Possum *Trichosurus vulpecula*

This is the most widely distributed and abundant of these large possum species but it was once much more widely distributed and abundant than it is now. It is very common in parts of some of our cities, Tasmania and Kangaroo Island and is an introduced and destructive pest in New Zealand. It has disappeared from large parts of the arid, semi-arid and tropical woodlands. Away from its urban haunts it is most likely to be found in open forests, woodlands and watercourses lined with river red gums.

Figure 4.1
Some of the early fox-like illustrations of the Common Brushtail Possum.
(a) 1827 from Griffith, Smith and Pigeon in *Animal Kingdom*
(b) 1846 from Waterhouse in *Natural History of Mammals*
(c) about 1880 from Desmarest in *Encyclopédie d'Histoire Naturelle*

It is very variable in colour and size throughout its extensive range. The 'typical race', as first described from the specimen found near Sydney and sent to England by Governor Phillip, is silver-grey on the back and white to pale grey underneath. The tapered tail is half grey and half black and thickly furred, except for the underside of the last third, which is naked. The ears are long and oval in shape. The adult weight of this 'typical' Brushtail (Plate 3) is around 1.6 to 2.4 kilograms and males are larger than females.

The first description and drawing of the Common Brushtail was published in 1789 in *The voyage of Governor Phillip to Botany Bay*, which was an account of 'all that is yet known of the Settlement at Sydney-Cove.' It was called the 'Vulpine Opossum' because of its apparent fox-like appearance — a reference to the pointed snout, long ears and bushy tail. In 1792 it was scientifically described by Kerr who used the fox likeness as the basis of the specific name *vulpecula,* which translates as 'little fox'. Many of the early drawings of this species relied a little too heavily on the fox analogy, producing some rather strange results(Figure 4.1).

The huge variation in body size, coat colour and furriness of the tail between populations of this species has long been recognised with some populations being raised to full species status at times and at least eight others being described as sub-species. The weight of adults varies from about one kilogram in the northern tropical regions of Australia to the large Tasmanian form, which can weigh more than three kilograms. Adults of most other populations generally weigh two to three kilograms. In addition to the most common silvery-grey colour of the original specimens, the coat ranges from the short-haired copper coloured form in central eastern Queensland to the very woolly almost black form found in Tasmania (Plate 4). The red colouring appears to be more common in the northern populations although older individuals also tend to become more reddish. In Tasmania there appears to be a habitat influence on coat colour with most black individuals occurring in the wetter habitats. Even amongst the larger southern forms of the Brushtail, there are many colours, with seven colour classes being recognised by the possum fur industry in New Zealand.

The three forms of the Common Brushtail Possum previously considered sufficiently distinctive to have been described as separate species are:

- Northern Brushtail Possum *T. arnhemensis*, from the Kimberley and Barrow Island in Western Australia and the Top End of the Northern Territory (Plate 5);
- Tasmanian Brushtail Possum *T. fuliginosus*; and
- Coppery Brushtail Possum *T. johnsoni*, from the Atherton Tableland in Queensland (Plate 6).

Genetic, morphological and captive breeding studies from populations throughout Australia indicate that there is only one species, *T. vulpecula*, which is highly variable in appearance but which has a surprisingly conservative genetic make-up. It also has a remarkable ecological flexibility when compared with other Australian marsupials.

Other populations have been described as sub-species, sometimes on the basis of incorrect information. The Mid-west Brushtail Possum *T. v. ruficollis* was described in 1909 from two specimens in the Frankfurt Zoological Gardens which were supposed to have come from the Murchison area of Western Australia but may have originated in Tasmania. The South-western Brushtail Possum, *T. v. hypoleucus* was described in 1855 from one specimen in Berlin, which was *thought* to have come from the south-west of Western Australia. Brushtails from Cape York were named *T. v. eburacensis* when they were discovered in 1916 because they were smaller, lighter and less furry and the Townsville Brushtail Possum was described as *T. v. mesurus*.

The Coppery Brushtail Possum may eventually be shown to be distinctive with further research. These are generally larger than the adjacent sclerophyll forest form and are predominantly red in colour. It has been suggested that, rather than being a form of the Common Brushtail, it may be more closely related to the Mountain Brushtail Possum. In the taxonomic analysis, these brushtails stood apart from adjacent populations with a consistent difference in the size of the first upper molar and two fixed enzyme differences but there was insufficient information to clearly resolve this problem.

Research in New Zealand has demonstrated that the possums introduced there have adapted to the local environment. There, skull size correlates with air temperature and for some populations this adaptation to the local environment took place within a short period of time — for some populations it occurred in only 30 generations.

COMMON BRUSHTAIL POSSUM Figure 4.2

Present
Past
(known since European settlement)
Pre-European
(evidence from sub-fossil/cave deposits)

Body size: Weight 1.2–4.5 kg;
Head/body length 350–550 mm;
Tail length 250–400 mm;
Ear length 50–60 mm.

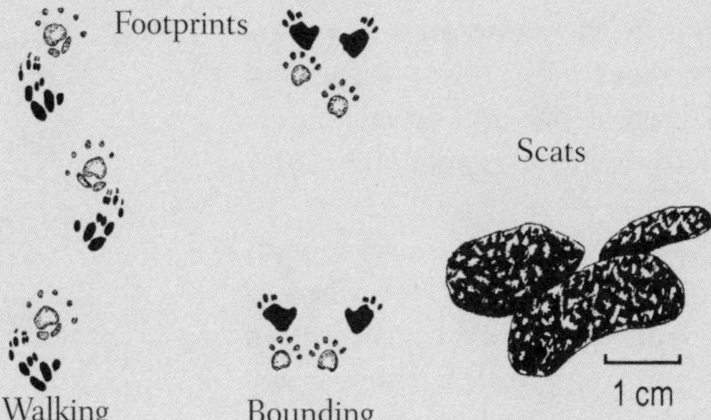

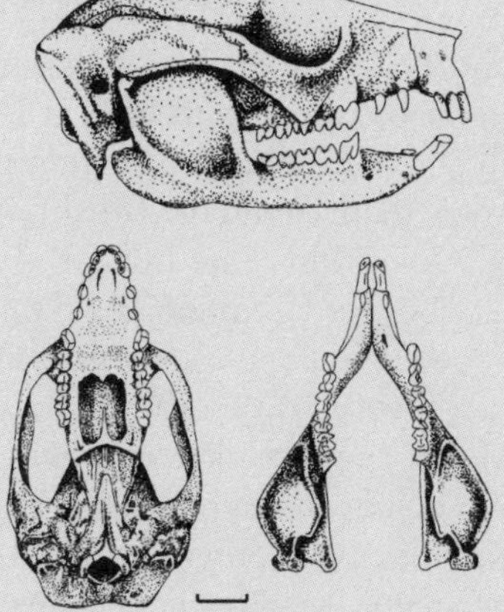

Finding the Common Brushtail Possum

TRACKS

- tracks show characteristic turned-out angle of the hind feet
- hind foot track has a clawless 'thumb'; — the two joined toes often only leave a single mark
- front foot has five evenly spaced toes
- foot placement differs between bounding and walking gait.

SCATS

- contain ground up plant fragments, usually hardened shiny surface, very occasionally insect fragments
- cylindrical, 1.5–2.0 centimetres long, 5 millimetres wide; slightly granulated surface; one end rounded, the other mostly pointed.

SHELTERS

- usually hollow limbs of trees or hollow logs, occasionally thick undergrowth
- bark and leaves used to line dens in breeding season
- nests in roofs of houses and sheds in urban and farming areas, also in parks and gardens and can use rock crevices in rocky areas.

OTHER SIGNS

- scratches on tree trunks.

Mountain Brushtail Possum *Trichosurus caninus* (Plate 7)

It took another 40 years to discover this species, which was first described as *Phalangista canina* by Ogilby in 1836. He continued the analogy between these possums and dogs by using the name *canina* (later changed to *caninus*), which means 'dog-like'. The original specimen was apparently collected by John Coxen, John Gould's brother-in-law, from 'country beyond the Hunter River ... north of Sydney'. This species was immediately considered to be distinctive from the Common Brushtail Possum because of its short and rounded ears. It has had several common names including Bobuck and Short-eared Brushtail Possum.

This species has a patchy distribution within the tall forests and rainforests of the Great Dividing Range and along the coast from south-eastern Queensland through New South Wales to the Port Phillip region of southern Victoria. In the north the preferred habitat includes dense subtropical rainforest, riverine vine thickets and even mangrove fringes. Further south it occupies temperate rainforest, wet sclerophyll forest and tall eucalypt forest.

The best way of distinguishing Mountain Brushtail Possums from a Common Brushtail is to look at the ears, which are about two-thirds the length and more rounded at the tip. Mountain Brushtail Possums are a little larger than Common Brushtails occurring in the same area weighing 2.5–4.5 kilograms. The tail fur also tends to taper more towards the end than it does for Common Brushtails. An analysis of size and colour differences between populations in NSW and Victoria suggests that there may be no contact between these populations.

Mostly they are olive or steely grey on the back but there is some variation in colour throughout their range. The blackish form was described as *Trichosurus caninus nigrans* in 1916 by Le Soeuf, who based his definition on specimens from the Tweed River area of New South Wales. These Black Bobucks have since been found throughout the distribution of this species and the definition of a sub-species is not justified. In some populations all animals are grey, in others there is a mixture of steel grey with olive grey, black, dark brown, coffee brown, and light grey in varying proportions. They are whitish on the front and frequently have deep yellow staining around the pouch and on the chest. The short, thick, woolly fur of the Mountain Brushtail is more dense than the fur of Common Brushtail Possums from the same area and was consequently preferred by trappers and furriers when they could be found.

MOUNTAIN BRUSHTAIL POSSUM Figure 4.3

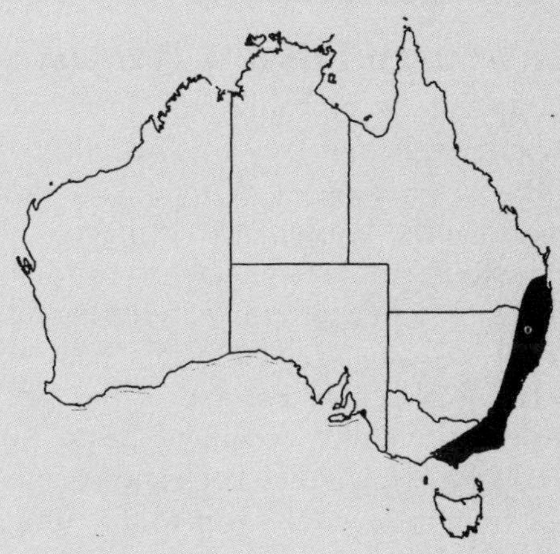

Body size: Weight 2.5–4.5 kg;
Head/body length 400–550 mm;
Tail length 340–420 mm;
Ear length 40–45 mm.
Skull and tracks like the Common Brushtail Possum.

Scats

Finding the Mountain Brushtail Possum

TRACKS

- tracks show characteristic turned-out angle of the hind feet and hind foot track has a clawless 'thumb' with the two joined toes often only leaving a single mark
- front foot has five evenly spaced toes
- foot placement differs between bounding and walking
- tracks larger than Common Brushtail's and stride longer but very difficult to separate.

SCATS

- contain ground up plant fragments, usually hardened shiny surface, very occasionally insect fragments
- cylindrical, 1.5–2.0 centimetres long, 5 millimetres wide; slightly granulated surface; one end rounded the other mostly pointed.

SHELTERS

- usually hollow limbs of trees or hollow logs, occasionally thick undergrowth
- bark and leaves used to line dens in breeding season.

OTHER SIGNS

- scratches on tree trunks.

Genus *Wyulda*

A single species restricted to Australia.

Scaly-tailed Possum *Wyulda squamicaudata*

This species is probably best known to the Aboriginal people of the Kimberley region of Western Australia so it is most appropriate that it has an Aboriginal name — Wyulda. Unfortunately this is a corruption of the name from the Western Desert people for the Brushtail Possum that can also be found in that area and was misapplied to this possum. The specific name is more appropriate, referring to the scaly appearance of the hairless tail — *squamicaudata* means 'scaly tail'.

The Scaly-tailed Possum is the size of a small Common Brushtail Possum with adults weighing 1.25 to 2.0 kilograms. The fur is pale grey, tipped with black on the back and cream on the underside. There is a dark stripe from between the ears to the rump, the base of the tail has a rufous tinge and the fur is yellow around the pouch. The tail is one of the most distinctive features of this possum. Fur continues onto the tail from the body and abruptly ends about a quarter of the way down. The skin on the remainder is raised into little scaly tubercles giving it a rasp-like appearance and each little tubercle is surrounded by a few short black bristles. There are no tubercles on the underside of the prehensile portion at the end of the tail. The head is a little broader and more flattened than the *Trichosurus* species and the muzzle is narrow and slender. The ears are rounded being only slightly longer than the width. The front feet reflect the largely terrestrial habit of this species with reduced claws sitting behind larger pads. Only the thumb is opposable.

Because of the remote location of its preferred habitat and its cryptic behaviour the Scaly-tailed Possum was not known scientifically until a live female was sent to the Perth Zoo in 1917, apparently from Violet Valley Aboriginal Reserve near Turkey Creek in the eastern Kimberley. Only two more specimens were collected — in 1942 and 1954 — prior to 1965 when biological surveys were begun in the Kimberley region. Several populations have now been found.

They seem to be restricted to the coastal edge of the western Kimberley, a very wet tropical area with a mean annual rainfall of more than 900 mm. No populations have been found near Turkey Creek which has a much drier climate, suggesting that the original specimen may not have come from there. They have quite specific habitat requirements, preferring rugged dissected sandstone country with boulders, a low open forest or woodland and some rainforest patches. They are thought to shelter deep in crevices between the boulders during the day, emerging to feed in the trees at night. If disturbed they quickly descend from the tree and hide amongst the boulders.

The Scaly-tailed Possum has been observed feeding on the leaves of several trees and on eucalyptus blossom. In captivity, it has been seen to extract seeds from a casuarina cone and to cache nuts. This behaviour combined with its large sectorial third premolar suggests that nuts may be an important food. Little is known about the breeding of this species but the young leave the pouch between 151 and 210 days and are probably not mature until their second year.

The cuscuses *Spilocuscus* and *Phalanger*

> Some animals resemble ferrets, only a little bigger. They are called kusus. They have a long tail with which they hang from the trees in which they live continuously, winding it once or twice around a branch. On their belly they have a pocket like an intermediate balcony; as soon as they give birth to a young one they grow inside there at a nipple until it does not need nursing any more. As soon as she has borne and nourished it, the mother becomes pregnant again. The people eat them like rabbits, seasoned with spices.

Figure 4.4
Scaly-tailed Possum

Nature Focus

Body size: Weight 1.35–2.0 kg;
Head/body length 310–395 mm;
Tail length 300 mm;
Ear length 30 mm.

This description was found in a Portuguese manuscript written in 1544 probably by the Portuguese Governor of the Moluccas (quoted by Calaby in Smith and Hume, 1984).

Cuscuses are an abundant, diverse group of phalangers. There are eighteen species within the three genera *Phalanger, Spilocuscus* and *Strigocuscus* found through Timor, Sulawesi, New Guinea and adjacent islands, and Cape York. The Bear Cuscus *Ailurops ursinus* is an uncommon species found only in Sulawesi and nearby islands. Cuscuses are very common in the New Guinean rainforests but the only two species found in Australia are restricted in their distribution and are uncommon. Until 1987 both species were included in the genus *Phalanger* that was first used by Buffon in 1765 to describe the fused second and third toes of the hind foot, forming the apparently two-clawed toe. At that time it was not known that this is a characteristic of all diprotodont marsupials. Because this was the first of the Australian possums to be named, the whole group is now known as the Phalangeridae.

The fur is short, woolly and dense and extends about half way down the prehensile tail. They vary in size from the Bear Cuscus which weighs up to 10 kilograms, has a head–body length of 610 mm and tail length of 525 mm, to the Small Sulawesi Cuscus (*Strigocuscus celebensis*) with a head/body length of 325–328 mm and tail length of 315–339 mm. Colour is also variable — the Mountain Cuscus (*Phalanger carmelitae*) is black and white, the Woodlark Cuscus (*Phalanger lullulae*) is mottled brown, ginger and white on the back and others are various combinations of grey, red, brown and white; males often differ from females in colour.

Genus *Spilocuscus*

A widely distributed genus with four species centering on New Guinea.

Common Spotted Cuscus *Spilocuscus maculatus* (Plate 8)

This is the more common of the two Australian cuscus species. It was first recorded as an Australian species in 1848 when Aboriginal people from the Port Albany area on Cape York gave one to John MacGillivray who was sailing on the HMS Rattlesnake. This specimen was described by John Gould as *Phalangista nudicaudata* and then renamed *Cuscus brevicauda* by Gray in 1858. Gould quickly recognised that his preceding name was inappropriate because the tails of all Cuscus species are naked on the end. Both of these descriptions were superseded as this species had already been described by the French natural historian Geoffroy as *Phalangista maculata*, the Brown-spotted Cuscus from the 'Moluccas' in 1804, but because he didn't publish the description as required, it was redescribed in 1818 by Desmarest using the same name.

It is found from the lowlands to altitudes above 1000 metres in New Guinea, on the Admiralty Islands and St Matthias group to the north, the southern Moluccas in the south west and on Cape York. It is the most widely distributed of the two Cuscus species in Australia but is restricted to forests from north of Coen to Lockerbie at the tip of the Cape and from sea level to the 820-metre summit of the McIlwraith Range. It is most common in the rainforests of the Iron Range but also can be seen up to half a kilometre from the rainforest into the eucalypt forests, in Nipa Palms of fringing mangroves, in freshwater and saline mangroves, and large paperbarks in riparian forest strips. In New Guinea and the Admiralty Islands, it is found in almost all habitats below 1200 metres altitude, except woodland and savannah.

On the east coast of Cape York there are three main populations — the McIlwraith Range–Iron Range, Jardine River and Lockerbie Scrub. There are also some populations in isolated patches of rainforest (<100 ha) in the middle of Cape York Peninsula and these may represent populations marooned by shrinking rainforest and now separated by totally unsuitable habitat. The long-term viability of these populations is precarious and although we know little about them, it seems that populations do not persist in habitat patches smaller than 200 hectares. In these isolates, the greater the distance from the nearest neighbouring patch and

Figure 4.5
Common
Spotted Cuscus

Body size:
Weight 1.35–2.0 kg;
Head/body length
310–395 mm;
Tail length 300 mm;
Ear length 30 mm.

Scats

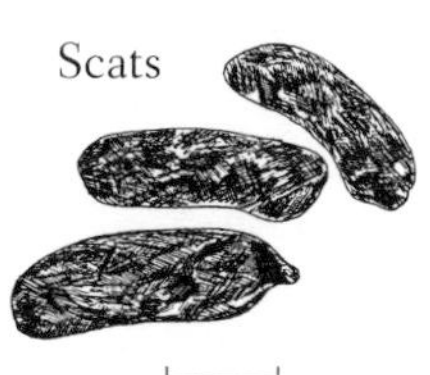

1 cm

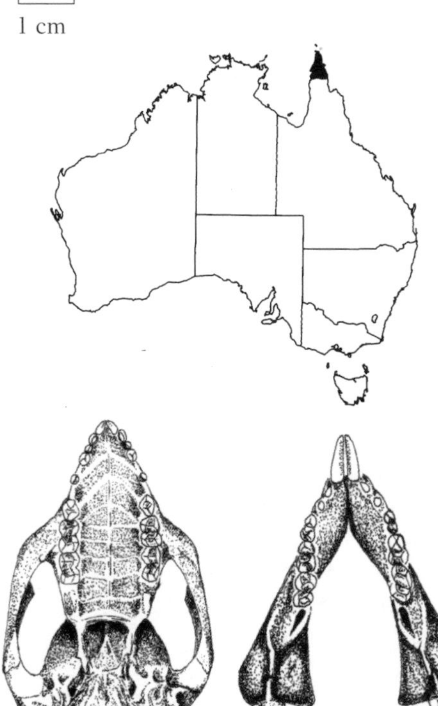

1 cm

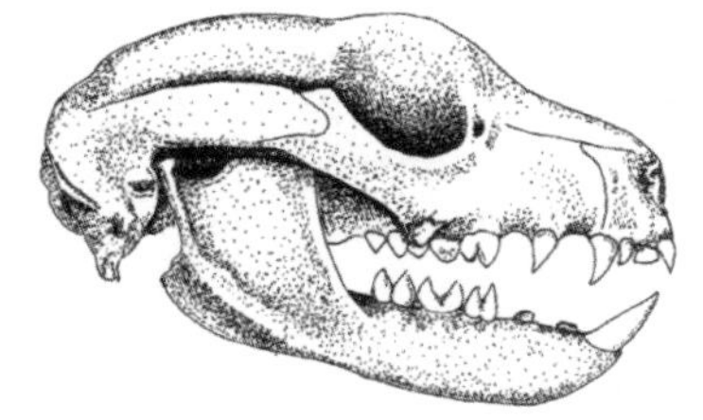

the more open the vegetation that animals have to cross, the less likely it is that they will be able to disperse between patches, and so the extinction of small populations is likely. In New Guinea they do not seem to mind disturbance, occurring in both primary and secondary rainforest formations as well as around large population centres.

Their ability to travel long distances on the ground, despite being an arboreal animal, and the fact that they don't require tree hollows for sleeping, may explain why they have a wider distribution on Cape York than does the Southern Common Cuscus. During the day they sleep on a branch or in a clump of foliage.

They eat a variety of fruits from rainforest trees such as the Leichhardt tree, native star apple (*Planchonella*) and figs, various flowers and some rainforest leaves. The relatively large canine teeth suggest a partly carnivorous diet and in captivity they readily take meat; there are reports of birds and other small animals being eaten.

These appealing round-faced animals have undoubtedly been the origin of reports of monkeys in Cape York. They are large, ranging from 1.5 to 4.9 kilograms and females are larger than males. The thick woolly fur is grey and white, the grey fur on the back of the males being blotched or marbled with white, while the female is generally grey, sometimes with a yellowish patch on the rump. The original description by Gould was undoubtedly of a juvenile female because he has illustrated a grey individual and notes that there was a light mark on the rump which he assumed resulted from their habit of sitting on the rump in the fork of a tree. They are white underneath, the tail fur is grey and the skin is pinkish-yellow. In New

Guinea they tend to be larger and the colour is more varied with the males having deep red-brown to blackish-brown blotches on a white background and the females being a darker grey. The small ears are thickly covered with fur, both inside and out.

The Australian Spotted Cuscus is not substantially different from the New Guinean form and the populations were probably continuous during the last land link ten thousand years ago. Several sub-species have been described with the Australian form being designated as *S. m. nudicaudatus* after the name given it by Gould.

Genus *Phalanger*

This genus occurs mostly in New Guinea and adjacent islands. There are 12 species.

SOUTHERN COMMON CUSCUS *PHALANGER INTERCASTELLANUS*

This species has had a confused taxonomic history in Australia since it was first discovered by G. Neuhauser in 1938 about 50 kilometres north of Coen in Queensland. It was described by Tate in 1945 who placed it as a subspecies *Phalanger orientalis peninsulae* of the Grey Cuscus. The Grey Cuscus, the species first recorded in the Moluccas was thought to be very variable and some ten sub-species were defined. It is now recognised as two distinct species and further division is possible. The Cape York populations belong to the new taxon *P. intercastellanus* named after the D'Entrecasteaux Islands of New Guinea where it was first found. The previous common name used for this species often led to its confusion with the grey females of the Common Spotted Cuscus. It also superficially resembles the Daintree River Ringtail. In New Guinea the fur colour varies between individuals; some are red underneath rather than white and some females are red on the back rather than grey.

In Australia the Southern Common Cuscus is readily distinguished from the Common Spotted Cuscus. The dark brown-grey fur has a distinctive dark brown stripe down the middle of the back, from between the ears to the rump. Males tend to become paler with age changing to an ashy brown colour on the back. Underneath they are a lighter, perhaps mottled colour and the females are white above the pouch. The snout is longer, the ears more prominent and only furred on the outside and it is a smaller more delicate animal with males weighing around 2 kilograms and females 1.5 kilograms. Like all cuscuses, the tail is two-thirds naked and this is the most reliable characteristic separating it from the Daintree River Ringtail Possum. It is a strongly prehensile tail with horny papillae on the naked underside.

This arboreal rainforest dweller is restricted to a single continuous population found in 188 890 hectares in the McIlwraith Range–Iron Range on the eastern side of Cape York Peninsula, from sea level to the range tops. It prefers the primary rainforest associations but can be found in wattles fringing the rainforest and vine-forest fringing the rivers. The absence of this species from any other rainforest areas on Cape York probably reflects its inability to cross open forest or woodland gaps as readily as the Common Spotted Cuscus.

They generally nest in tree hollows during the day so they are hard to find, which may be why they were not found in Australia until 1938. In New Guinea they shelter amongst tree foliage during the day as well as in hollows. When active, they are not as cryptic in behaviour as the Common Spotted Cuscus, making them easier to spotlight, especially with their bright red eye-shine. They do not spend much time on the ground, moving confidently through the canopy and often leaping between branches.

Outside Australia they occur in the southern half of New Guinea, along the eastern coast and on several islands. They are generally common, especially in the D'Entrecasteaux Islands and near gardens and villages where forest regrowth and plantations provide ample food. In Australia they eat the green fruits of the red cedar, flowers of the corky bark *Carallia brachiata* and various tree leaves. The stomach of one individual was found to be filled with a paste apparently derived from black bean. They are not so interested in meat in captivity as the Common Spotted Cuscus.

Figure 4.6
Southern Common Cuscus

Body size:
Weight 1.5–2.2 kg;
Head/body length 350–400 mm;
Tail length 280–350 mm;
Ear length 25–26 mm.

PSEUDOCHEIRIDAE

Genus *Hemibelideus*

One Australian species.

Lemuroid Ringtail Possum *Hemibelideus lemuroides*

This is one of several possum species found in the high altitude rainforests of north Queensland. It is not distinctive, mostly being distinguished by appearing as a chocolate brown ball high in the canopy at night. It is strictly nocturnal, spending the day in a tree hollow. When looking for this possum you are most likely to hear the crash landings it makes as it jumps between branches before you see it. It is rarely found less than about ten metres above the ground. They are generally much more agile and active than other ringtail species.

Most individuals are charcoal-brown on the back with a reddish-brown tinge on the shoulders, yellowish underneath and a black tail. Fawn individuals are also found and Longman described these as the species *Hemibelideus cervinus* in 1915. They are now known to be just a colour variation that is fawn above and below with a tinge of orange on the shoulders and a lighter fawn head. The face is short and broad and the short ears do not project much beyond the long fur. The prehensile tail is about the same length as the head and body, is somewhat bushy with only a slight taper and the short bare area underneath ends in a completely bare finger-like tip. Adults produce a distinctive, penetrating musky odour.

The apparent affinities between this species and the small gliders (Petauridae) led Collett, who described it in 1884, to believe that it was a transitional form between ringtails and gliders so he placed them in the subgenus *Hemibelideus* which means 'semi-glider'. The specific name *lemuroid* refers to the striking similarity with the lemur monkeys, especially the short snout and forward facing eyes. It has several similarities with the Greater Glider especially the soft, woolly fur and the long, almost fully furred tail. They also spread their limbs widely like a glider when they jump even though they do not have any gliding membranes. David Fleay demonstrates some of this thinking in his book *Gliders of the Gum Trees* where he states:

> In northern Queensland there lives one of the Ringtails, from which group the largest Glider undoubtedly arose, that possesses not only a plume-like tail but the merest rudimentary ridge of gliding membrane along its flanks. This animal (*Hemibelideus lemuroides* — literally, semi-glider like a lemur) indulges in extensive downward and outward leaps. Consequently it is some distance along the way to development as a volplaning type.

The first specimens were collected by Carl Lumholtz between Cardwell and the Herbert River in Queensland. They are now found in continuous rainforest above an altitude of 450 metres between Ingham and Cairns and to the west of Mossman above 1100 metres on the Mount Carbine

Tableland. Unfortunately they do not seem to be able to survive in small rainforest remnants, eventually disappearing from patches less than 80 hectares in size. Lemuroid Ringtail Possums are quite social, frequently being seen in pairs or family groups. Densities can be quite high with records of 2–5 per spotlight hour being common and up to 10 per hour in habitat above an altitude of 900 metres.

Figure 4.7 Lemuroid Ringtail Possum

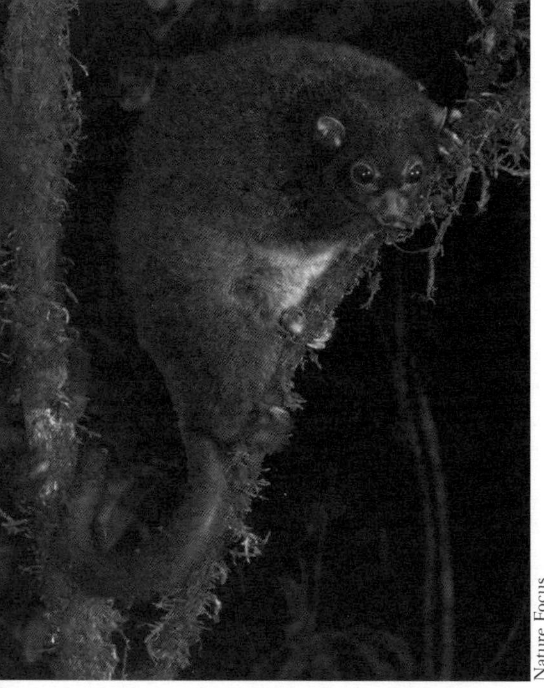

Nature Focus

Body size:
Weight 810–1060 g males and 750–1140 g females;
Head/body length 344 mm males and 342 mm females;
Tail length 300–373 mm;
Ear length 22–25 mm;
Distinctive Feature: Brilliant white yellow eye shine.

Genus *Petauroides*

One Australian species.

Greater Glider *Petauroides volans* (Plate 9)

The Greater Glider was discovered by naturalists from the First Fleet and described as the 'Black Flying Opossum' in Governor Phillip's account of the colony published in 1789. This description was then used by Kerr to name the species *Didelphis volans* in 1792. In his account, Phillip remarked on the beauty and fine quality of the fur, noting that 'it might probably be thought a very valuable article of commerce' if abundantly available. This species is common but fortunately for the Greater Glider the presumed value of the fur was not realised because it is too soft and does not remain in the skin when tanned.

When it was first discovered, the Greater Glider was recognised as a marsupial and not thought to be related to the placental Flying Squirrels as were the small gliders (*Petaurus* species), but its similarity with the Malayan Flying Squirrel led to it being known as the 'Taguan Glider' at one time and given the specific name of *Petaurista taguanoides* by Gould. Throughout its early scientific history, the taxonomy was confused — it was redescribed several times as additional specimens were collected and sometimes considered to be the same species as the Yellow-bellied Glider (*Petaurus australis*). In 1934 it was mistakenly assigned the generic name *Schoinobates* but this name was originally used for one of the Flying Squirrels (Sciuridae) rather than a marsupial.

The scientific name *Petauroides volans* is very apt, translating as 'flying rope-walker'. Greater Gliders are quite agile when climbing but are extremely clumsy and slow when on the ground. They are graceful and skilled when gliding, being able to cover distances of up to 100 metres and to change direction by perhaps 90 degrees in one glide. The flight is downwards but just before landing on the trunk of the tree, the trajectory sweeps gently upwards, they lose momentum and clasp the trunk with all four feet. Their gliding ability is well demonstrated in this description by Troughton (1941):

> One animal in six successive glides was once observed to cover a distance of 590 yards [540 metres], when a resident at Milton, New South Wales saw a Glider in the twilight near his home leave the top of a eucalypt 100 feet high and glide to the foot of another 70 yards away; this it immediately climbed and from the summit glided to the next at 80 yards, and lost no time in ascending three more trees at distances of 110, 120, and 90 yards, finally gliding to another 120 yards away in which it remained.

Individuals will repeatedly use the same routes as they move from their nest hollows to feed.

Early references to 'parachute-like membranes' are not appropriate but it is difficult to know if the description by David Fleay of gliding 'like an aerial frying pan with the long tail streaming out behind' is any better! The shape of the gliding membrane (patagium) and the way of gliding differs substantially between the Greater Glider and the small gliders (Petauridae) (see Figure 3.4).

The long silky fur and long fully furred tail tend to make Greater Gliders seem larger than their 1.0–1.5 kilograms. Most are dark grey on the back, whitish underneath and have a dark grey tail, giving rise to the other common name of Dusky Glider. The large ears are thickly covered by dark fur outside and are naked inside. Colour is variable and about 5 per cent of animals are pale. These have differing proportions of cream colour ranging from smoky-grey flanks, mottled grey back, grey back with cream head and tail to cream all over. This variation in colour is found through most populations regardless of habitat, although it is less common in the smaller northern glider populations. Two sub-specific forms of the Greater Glider have been described: *Petauroides volans volans*, is larger and found from Victoria to about the Tropic of Capricorn and *P. v. minor* occurs north of the Tropic of Capricorn. While they are currently regarded only as forms of the one species they may be distinct species.

The Greater Glider is a common species found in a variety of eucalypt forest types from central Victoria to about Cairns in Queensland, from the coast to the western slopes of the Divide. It can be quite abundant and easy to find with its bright eyeshine and habit of sitting staring from high in a tree.

Plate 1
'Ascending the tallest trees after the opossum and flying squirrel.' Painting by John Heaviside Clark in his *Field Sports of the Native Inhabitants of New South Wales*, 1813 (Mitchell Library, State Library of New South Wales)

Plate 2
'Smoking out the opossum.' Painting by John Heaviside Clark in his *Field Sports of the Native Inhabitants of New South Wales*, 1813 (*Mitchell Library, State Library of New South Wales*)

Plate 3
Common Brushtail Possum—south-eastern form
(*Ray and Anne Williams*)

Plate 4
Variation in the appearance of the Common Brushtail Possum
(*illustrated by Neville Cayley in Troughton 1948*)

5 5A 3

2 4 1

Plate 5
(opposite page top)
Common Brushtail Possum—
northern form
(*Anne Kerle*)

Plate 6
(opposite page bottom)
Common Brushtail Possum—
coppery form
(*Anne Kerle*)

Plate 7
Mountain Brushtail Possum
(*Ray and Anne Williams*)

Plate 8
Common Spotted Cuscus
(*Nature Focus*)

Plate 9
Greater Glider
(*Sue Brookhouse*)

Plate 10
(opposite page)
Common Ringtail Possum
(*Ray and Anne Williams*)

Plate 11
Common Ringtail Possum—red form
(*Ray and Anne Williams*)

Plate 12
(opposite page)
Western Ringtail Possum
(*Ric Howe*)

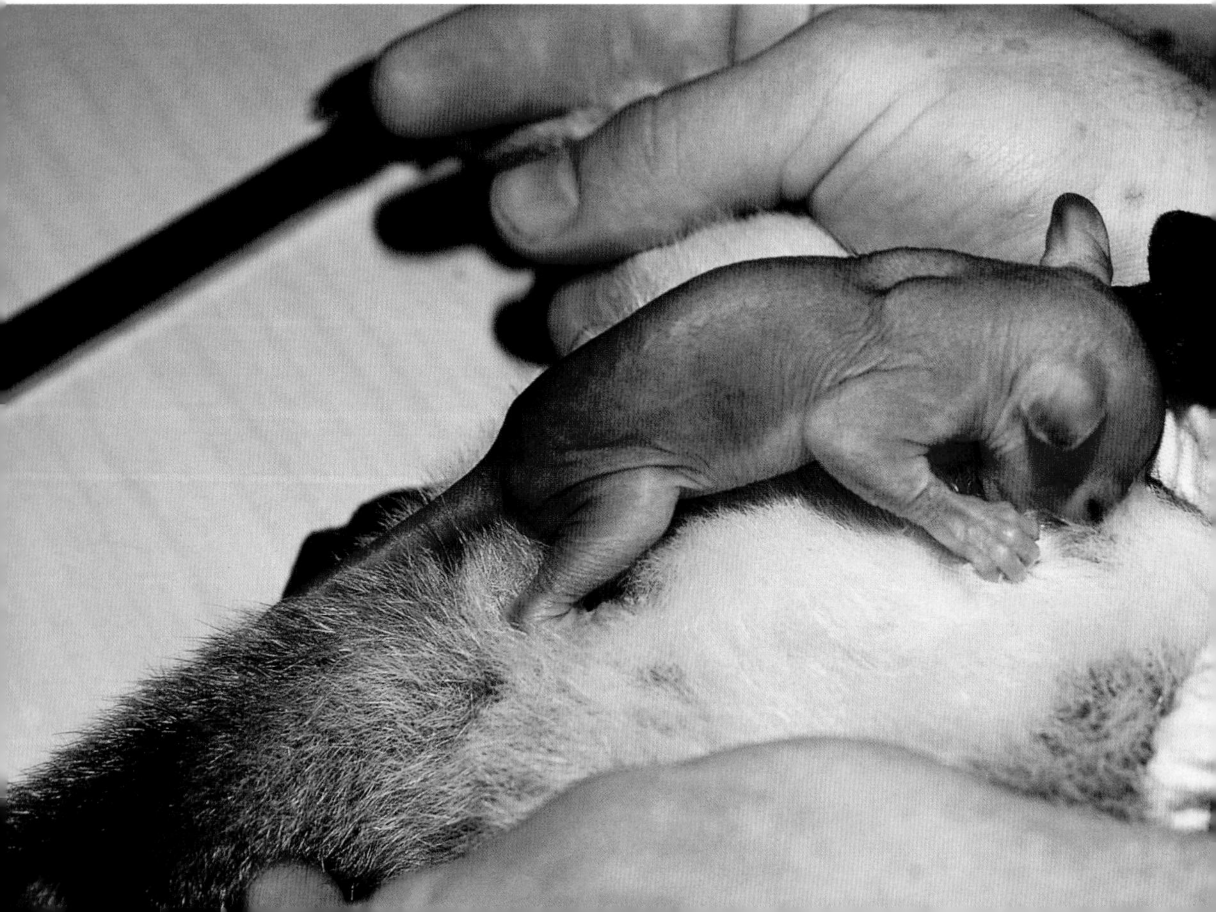

Plate 13
(opposite page top)
Northern Brushtail Possum Pouch young—41 days old
(*Anne Kerle*)

Plate 14
(opposite page bottom)
Northern Brushtail Possum Pouch young—96 days old
(*Anne Kerle*)

Plate 15
(top)
Northern Brushtail Possum Pouch young—
120 days old
(*Anne Kerle*)

Plate 16
(bottom)
Northern Brushtail Possum Pouch young—
136 days old
(*Anne Kerle*)

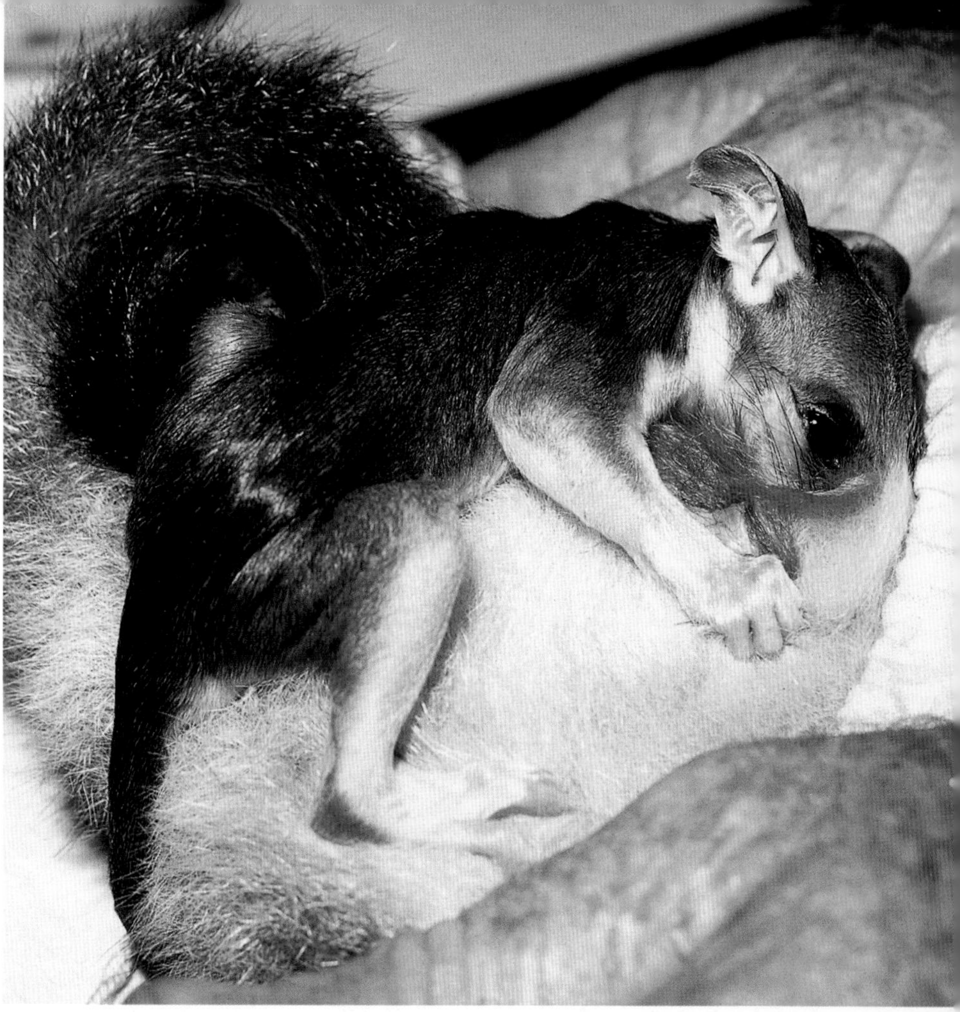

Plate 17
(top) Common Brushtail Possum six months old, still suckling (*Anne Kerle*)
(left) Northern Brushtail Possum six months old, still suckling (*Anne Kerle*)

Plate 18
A rocky platform heavily marked with paracloacal secretions by the Rock Ringtail Possum (*Anne Kerle*)

GREATER GLIDER Figure 4.8

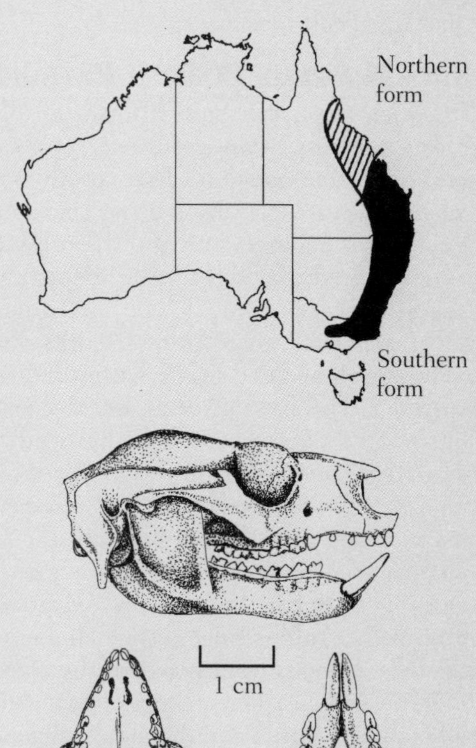

Body size:
Southern form weight 900–1700 g;
Head/body length 350–450 mm;
Tail length 450–600 mm;
Ear length 44–46 mm;
Northern form weight 750g;
Head/body length 300–380 mm;
Tail length 418–450 mm;
Ear length 30–35 mm.

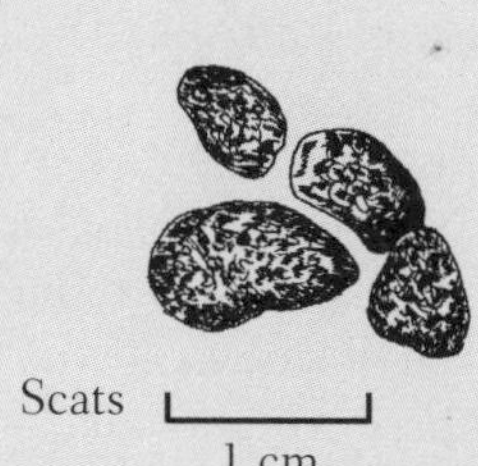

Finding the Greater Glider

TRACKS
- Greater Gliders spend little time on the ground
- hind foot has a clawless opposable toe like other possums
- front feet have two inner toes at an angle to the other three as in ringtails.

SCATS
- similar to Common Ringtail but smaller and less granulated
- contain ground up plant fragments, very occasionally insect fragments
- found at the base of trees.

SHELTERS
- tree hollows, often in large, dead trees, entry hole usually high up in the trunk, sometimes lined with leaves and strips of bark.

OTHER SIGNS
- scratches on tree trunks
- eyeshine: glowing jewel-like orbs.

Genus *Petropseudes*

One Australian species.

Rock Ringtail Possum *Petropseudes dahli*

The Rock Ringtail Possum differs from all other Ringtail Possums by being mostly terrestrial, living exclusively in rocky outcrops with deeply fissured rocks and large boulders. This strictly nocturnal species shelters deep in cracks and caves during the day and emerges to feed from various tree species growing in and around the rocky habitat. Often these possums do not even need to climb to feed, being able to reach their food from rock ledges. They apparently do not build a nest and can occasionally be found sleeping on well-protected rock ledges during the day.

It is well adapted to life within the rugged rocky country of northern Australia. The most striking adaptations are the proportionally shorter tail, which is only about half the head-body length; short strong limbs; and stocky build. The first two digits of the hand are not as obviously opposable to the other three, the claws are short and there are differences in the shape of the skull such as the narrow pointed muzzle and the deeply concave region between the eyes which is bordered by sharp parallel ridges. It has thick woolly fur, grizzled or silvery grey on the back, often with a rufous tinge, especially on the rump and tail. A darker dorsal stripe extends from between the eyes to the middle of the back. The underneath is a paler creamy colour. About half of the short prehensile tail is thickly furred and the almost naked end can be held almost at right angles to the rest of the tail. The bare portion is not scaly like the Scaly-tailed Possum.

The Rock Ringtail was not known scientifically until 1895 when it was located after some persistent searching by the Norwegian collector Knut Dahl. He had been alerted to the existence of this species by Aboriginal informants but initially believed it to be some form of tree kangaroo. After considerable effort by his Aboriginal assistants three were located — two adults and a juvenile — deep within the granite boulders near the upper reaches of the Mary River in the Northern Territory. Dahl erroneously considered the local Aboriginal people to be less than human, but his scientific endeavours would have failed without their knowledge and assistance. The species was described by the Norwegian zoologist Robert Collett as *Pseudocheirus dahli* but in 1923 was considered sufficiently distinctive by Oldfield Thomas to be placed into its own genus of *Petropseudes*, which simply translates as 'rock possum'.

Little was known about the distribution, abundance and biology of this species until quite recently. In addition to the specimens collected by Dahl, twenty-four specimens were collected from the South Alligator River area of the Northern Territory by J. T. Tunney in 1903–4 and the species was thought to be restricted to the sandstone and granite uplands of western Arnhem Land until the 1940s. It is probably most abundant in this region but is also found in the Kimberleys, on Groote Eylandt, in the

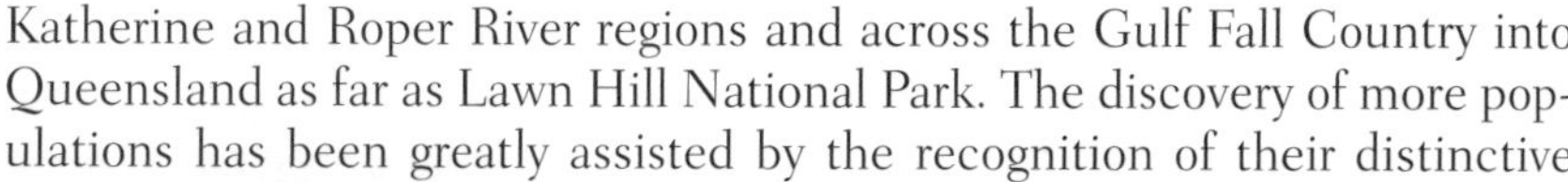

Figure 4.9
Rock Ringtail Possum

Katherine and Roper River regions and across the Gulf Fall Country into Queensland as far as Lawn Hill National Park. The discovery of more populations has been greatly assisted by the recognition of their distinctive scats, which appear to be common within their preferred habitat, but this is patchy; populations are not always present in apparently suitable habitat.

Nature Focus

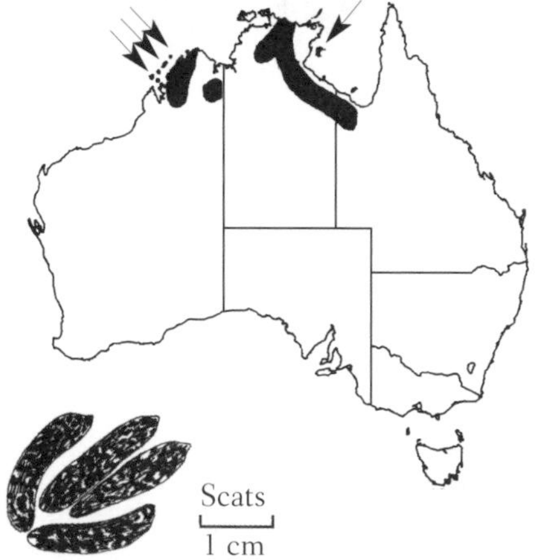

Body size:
Weight 1.28–2.0 kg;
Head/body length 334–375 mm males and 349–383 mm females;
Tail length 200–220 mm males, and 207–266 mm females;
Ear length 26–31 mm.

The scats of this possum are very distinctive being reddish brown or black with a slightly bent cigar shape, 15–25 mm long and about 5 mm wide. The eyeshine is very bright but the animals usually do not freeze when caught in the spotlight beam. Mostly they are unlikely to be confused with other possums but populations of Northern Brushtail Possums may be found in nearby tropical open forest and Rock Ringtails have been found in the same area as some Scaly-tailed Possums in the western Kimberleys.

Genus *Pseudochirops*

This genus is mostly found in New Guinea where there are four species, one of which is also in Australia. The first of this genus to be discovered was D'Albertis' Ringtail *Pseudochirops albertisii*. Very little is known about the biology of the New Guinean *Pseudochirops* species.

GREEN RINGTAIL POSSUM *PSEUDOCHIROPS ARCHERI*

This, the most solitary of the Australian Ringtail Possums, was first described by Collett in 1884. It is a particularly attractive animal. The crimped guard hairs have fine alternating bands of black, yellow and white giving a peculiar glossy green appearance that blends well with the surrounding vegetation. There are two silvery stripes along the back separated by narrow darker stripes and the white patches behind the ears and under the eyes are quite distinctive. The underside, inside of the legs and the end third of the tail are also white. The strongly prehensile tail is thick at the base, tapered to the tip and a little shorter than head-body length.

The Green Ringtail, also known as the Striped Ringtail, is found in dense upland rainforests from near Townsville to the Mount Windsor Tableland west of Mossman. It does not occur below an altitude of about 300 metres. The Herbert River and Lemuroid Ringtails are also found in the same high altitude rainforests. The Green Ringtail sleeps on a branch amongst foliage rather than in a tree hollow or nest and if disturbed will move around during the day. It rests curled in a tight ball, gripping a branch with the hindfeet and sitting on the base of the coiled tail. It will also assume this posture when surprised at night but retreats rapidly along the branches as soon as it can. It rarely descends to the ground. Their ability to run quickly from tree to tree was noted by Carl Lumholtz who collected the first specimens, remarking that Aboriginal people had difficulty killing them unless there were two or three people stationed in different trees.

Figure 4.10 Green Ringtail Possum

Ray & Anne Williams

Body size:
Weight 1064 g males and 1119 g females;
Head/body length 353 mm males and 335 mm females;
Tail length 330 mm males, and 325 mm females;
Ear length 23–26 mm.

The original specimens were collected from the Lower Herbert River where they were quite common and many were collected from the Bellenden Ker Range. They are now sparse within their preferred habitat. Parts of their habitat have been cleared but the remainder is included in the Wet Tropics World Heritage area. They are generally solitary although occasionally a mother and young may be seen together and even more rarely, a male and female. They make almost no vocalisations.

High altitude ringtail possums *Pseudochirulus* species

Until recently the two Australian species of this genus were considered as only subspecifically distinct. There are five more species found in New Guinea. As with most ringtails, very little is known about the biology of the New Guinean species.

Daintree Ringtail Possum *Pseudochirulus cinereus*

The Daintree Ringtail was classified as a northern pale coloured form of the Herbert River Ringtail Possum until 1989 when chromosome studies demonstrated that they are a distinct species. The name *cinereus*, which translates as 'ash-coloured little pseudocheirus', was first used by Tate in 1945. They are similar in colour to the juveniles of the Herbert River Ringtail, being caramel-fawn on the back with a dark stripe from between the eyes to the lower back and creamy white underneath. The darker tail is prehensile, tapering, naked along almost the entire underside and usually white on the last third. The juveniles are generally paler in colour.

There are only three separate populations of this species on Thornton Peak, Mount Windsor Tableland and Mount Carbine Tableland in Queensland. They occupy wet tropical rainforests above an altitude of 420 metres. The first specimens were found on Mount Spurgeon at 1200 metres. Populations are more dense at higher altitudes, especially above 1000 metres. Relatively little is known about this species. It is generally solitary and consumes a variety of leaves, the fruits of several figs and probably other fruits. It is thought to nest in tree hollows but is also known to sleep on exposed branches.

Figure 4.11 Daintree Ringtail Possum

Nature Focus

Body size:
Weight 1092 g males and 908 g females;
Head/body length 353 mm males and 352 mm females;
Tail length 360 mm males, and 344 mm females;
Ear length 20–27 mm.
Distinctive feature: Bright red eye shine.

Herbert River Ringtail Possum *Pseudochirulus herbertensis*

The Herbert River Ringtail was first found by Carl Lumholtz in the upper mountain forests of the Herbert River Gorges west of Cardwell in Queensland and described by Collett in 1884. A 'swamp race' of this species, *P. h. colletti,* was previously described but this subspecies is no longer recognised.

This very distinctive possum is dark, almost black on the back and white on the chest, belly and upper forearms. The amount of white is variable with some individuals having almost none. Unlike the co-existing Lemuroid Ringtail, the Herbert River Ringtail has a tapered tail which is dark and densely furred at the base and white with short hairs for the last 25–110 mm. Underneath the tail is naked and rough for two-thirds of its length. The short pinkish-white ears do not project much beyond the thick woolly fur. Juveniles are ginger or pale brown rather than dark brown or black on the back.

The Herbert River Ringtail has a limited distribution, being restricted to rainforest above about 350 metres between the Mount Lee area to the west of Ingham and the Lamb Range west of Cairns. It occurs sparsely, with population densities of 0.5 to 3.0 possums per hour of spotlighting. It can occasionally be found in the fringing forests of Flooded Gum on the western edge of the rainforests.

Figure 4.12 Herbert River Ringtail Possum

Body size:
Weight 1177 g males and 1053 g females;
Head/body length 370 mm males and 344 mm females;
Tail length 373 mm males, and 363 mm females.

It is strictly nocturnal like the Lemuroid Ringtail and generally solitary like the Green Ringtail. All three species can be found in the same area. Being a strongly arboreal but cautious climber, it rarely descends below 6 metres above the ground and moves between the trees along the branches; rather than leaping it will grip the branch strongly with the prehensile tail and hind feet and stretch the body across the gap between branches. Vine tangles, tree holes or fern clumps high in trees provide the nests. The young remain on the back for about two weeks and are then left in dense foliage or in the nest. It eats leaves almost exclusively but some fruits and flowers may be included at times. Leaves are eaten from a variety of tree species but those with a higher proportion of protein are often preferred.

Ringtail possums *Pseudocheirus* species

The ringtail possums are well named. They have a long, slender tapered tail with the tip being frequently curled into a ring. The scientific name of the genus was first proposed by Ogilby in 1837 to replace *Didelphis* originally used by Boddaert. Its meaning, 'false-hand', refers to the appearance of the front feet, which have the two inner toes opposable to the other three. This characteristic is also found in other possums (except brushtails) and the Koala so it is not a distinctive feature of this genus.

The number of species has varied greatly since *Didelphis peregrinus* was described in 1785 — some have been split into their own genus while others have been lumped in with *Pseudocheirus peregrinus*. As with the Common Brushtail Possum, there is variation in size and colour between populations throughout their distribution and there was also early confusion about where specimens were collected. For example, the specimen which Desmarest used to describe *Phalangista cookii* in 1818 was collected by the French naturalists Peron and Leseur near Sydney but most workers assumed it had come from Tasmania or even northern New South Wales. *Phalangista convolutor* was described from the possums recorded on James Cook's third voyage from Adventure Bay in Tasmania and was long considered to be sufficiently distinct to remain as a separate species. Taxonomic studies have not supported this separation despite Le Soeuf even describing the Flinders Island population as a sub-species of *P. convolutor*. In all, sixteen species have been described, most of which are no longer valid.

Common Ringtail Possum *Pseudocheirus peregrinus* (Plate 10)

The Common Ringtail Possum is often seen although it is not as well recognised as the bolder Common Brushtail Possum. The two are frequently confused especially in the urban environment where the smaller ringtails prefer to nest in dense bush remnants rather than around buildings and rarely become a nuisance, although they do enjoy dining on rosebuds and fruit trees.

There is considerable geographic variation in coat colour with darker forms occurring in coastal and rainforest habitats and paler grey forms in drier inland open forests. John Gould reported that the Aboriginal people in the Hunter Valley

> particularly impressed upon my attention that the animal from the flats was different from the one frequenting the brushes which clothe the 'corries' of the great Liverpool chain.

Most commonly they are silver-grey, smoky-grey or dark grey-brown on the back and sides, cream or grey underneath, reddish or tan on the arms and legs. They can also be light grey or rich red on the back (Plate 11). The tapering tail is white on the lower portion (varying from half to a third of the length) and abruptly changes to dark grey nearer the body. The short ears have a white patch at the back.

The Common Ringtail Possum can be found along the east coast, including all of Cape York and extending through Victoria and south-eastern South Australia to Adelaide, from the coast to the western slopes of the Great Dividing Range. It is also found in Tasmania. There are four subspecies: the populations from most of Queensland, inland NSW and Victoria and South Australia are *P. p. peregrinus*; populations from south-eastern Queensland and north coastal NSW are *P. p. pulcher*; the coastal populations from southern NSW and Victoria are *P. p. cooki*; and the Tasmanian form is *P. p. convolutor*. It is possible that these may represent a group of closely related species, still in the process of separating. The specific name *peregrinus* translates as 'from foreign parts', a reference to its first description as *Didelphis* (the American Opossums), which was known only from distant lands. Their preferred habitat ranges from rainforests to mangroves, tea-tree scrub, eucalypt forests and woodlands.

COMMON RINGTAIL POSSUM Figure 4.13

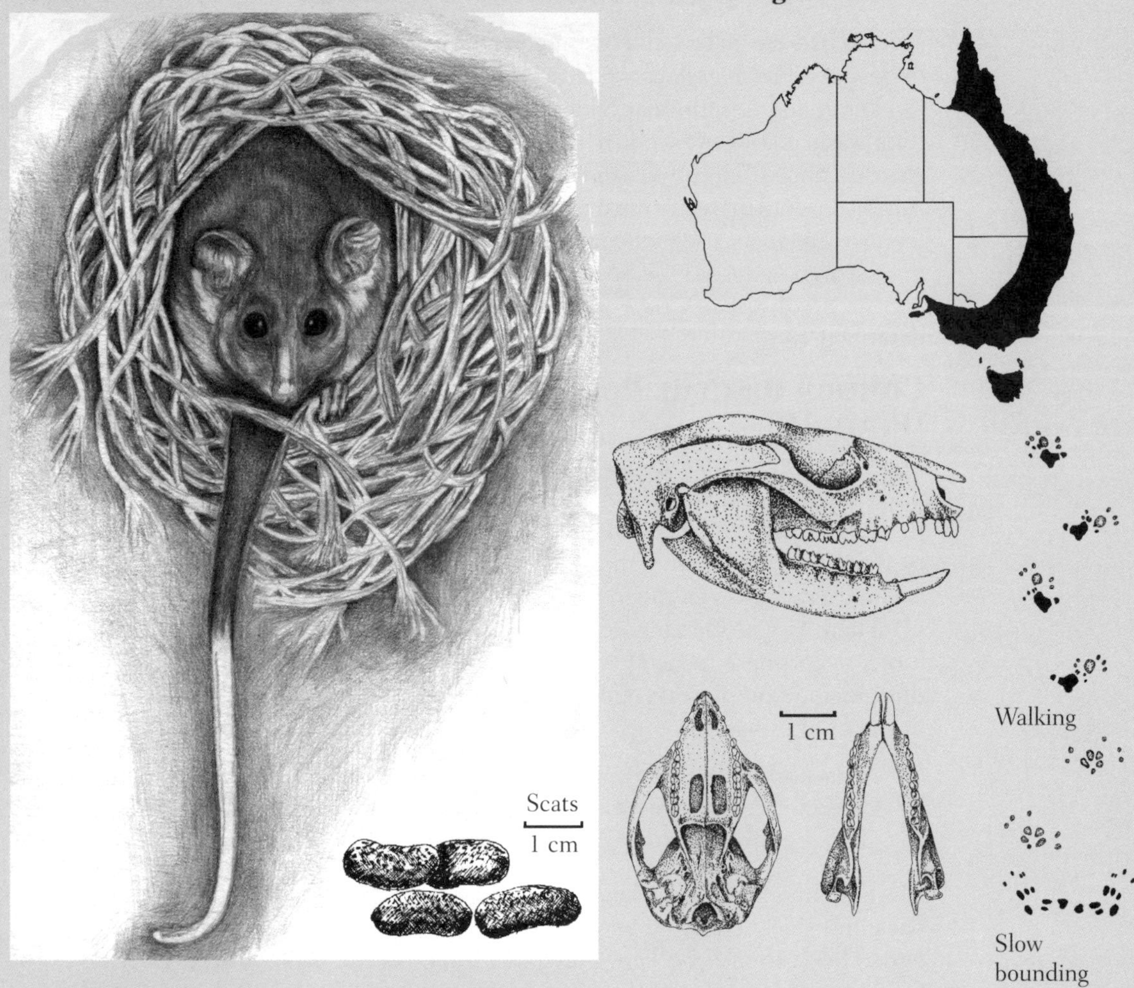

Body size: Southern specimens: Weight 700–1100 g; Head/body length 300–350 mm; Tail length 300–350 mm; Ear length 35–40 mm; Northern specimens: Weight 660–880 g; Head/body length 300–344 mm; Tail length 317–381 mm.

Finding the Common Ringtail Possum

TRACKS

- distinguished from brushtails by the different spread of toes on front feet — ringtails have the two inner toes at an angle to the other three
- foot placement differs between bounding and walking gait.

SCATS

- contain ground up plant fragments, very occasionally insect fragments
- cylindrical <1.5–2.0 cm long, <5 mm wide, smaller than Common Brushtail Possum's; granulated surface, rounded on both ends, often reddish in colour.

SHELTERS

- nests in tree hollows or builds a drey
- the drey is a bulky, roughly spherical ball, about 25–30 cm across, made of twigs, strips of bark, leaves, ferns and grasses; entrance hole 8–10 cm diameter in one side; usually built in a fork or among the branches of a tree or shrub.
- may also nest in mistletoe clumps and roofs of sheds and houses.

OTHER SIGNS

- scratches on tree trunks.

Ric How

Figure 4.14
Western
Ringtail Possum

Present
Past
Pre-European

Body size:
Weight 900 g males and 1100 g females;
Head/body length 300 mm males and 400 mm females;
Tail length 300 mm males, and 400 mm females.

WESTERN RINGTAIL POSSUM *PSEUDOCHEIRUS OCCIDENTALIS* (PLATE 12)

This close western relative of the Common Ringtail Possum was first described from a specimen collected by John Gilbert for Gould from King George Sound near Albany and described by Oldfield Thomas in 1888. It was not described as a new species but rather it was thought to be the same as the Tasmanian Ringtail *P. convolutor*. Since then the species has been variously named as the western subspecies of the Common Ringtail Possum or as a full species. The name *occidentalis* simply means 'western', referring to its distribution.

They are very similar to the Common Ringtail in eastern Australia but generally larger and darker with some being a very dark grey on the back. They are cream or grey underneath, the ears are short and rounded and the white section on the tail tip is of variable length. They weigh around one kilogram.

This species has declined greatly since European settlement and since 1983 has been considered rare and endangered. Analysis of sub-fossil deposits, historical specimen records and early surveys show that it previously occurred across most of the south west of the state. It is now found only in the near-coastal area from Bunbury to Albany, the Swan coastal plain near Busselton, parts of urban Busselton and inland in the Perup area of the Warren River Catchment. In some parts of the present range it can be quite abundant.

The reason for the decline, first noted in 1909, is most likely to be clearing of the preferred habitat in association with predation by foxes. Gilbert, who collected the original specimen, considered this species to be unusual because it could be found living on the ground:

> ...it does not confine itself to the hollows of the trees, but is often found in holes in the ground, where the entrance is covered by a stump, from which it is often hunted out by the kangaroo dogs. It varies very much in the colour of the fur, from a very light grey to nearly black. In one instance I caught a pair in the same hole exhibiting these extremes of colour. (Troughton 1941)

Recent workers have found them to be difficult to capture because they rarely come to the ground or enter traps. Perhaps this perceived change in behaviour reflects an adaptation for evading further depredation by foxes.

Finding the Western Ringtail Possum

See Common Ringtail Possum.

WHERE POSSUMS LIVE

The distribution or geographical range of each of the large possum species across Australia varies considerably from the Common Brushtail Possum, which has the widest occurrence of any Australian mammal, to the Southern Common Cuscus, found in only a few thousand hectares. But distribution maps tell only part of the story. Special requirements for feeding, nesting or breeding generally mean that populations will only live in a portion of the area represented by a distribution map and that population density will vary across their geographical range. The Common Brushtail, Mountain Brushtail, Common Ringtail and Greater Glider all have an overlapping distribution but are not necessarily found in the same place — each species has different habitat requirements within that distribution.

Knowing the habitat preferences of possum species is the first step in being able to find one in the wild. This knowledge is also critical for effective conservation. The habitats and the variation in population size are described here for each of the four most common species and the Western Ringtail.

HABITAT SELECTION

A habitat must have suitable resources for shelter (either hollows or materials to build nests), quality food resources and adequate water. These are not evenly distributed through the forests or woodlands. This has been shown by a detailed study by CSIRO of all arboreal fauna in the tall eucalypt forests of the south coast of New South Wales, which found that 63 per cent of possums lived in about 9 per cent of the available forest. In this study there was a positive association between possum densities and the levels of the micronutrients potassium, nitrogen, and phosphorus in leaves and soil.

Eucalypts also contain anti-herbivore or anti-nutritional compounds: phenols, essential oils, and lignins. These defence compounds may be produced by the tree at higher levels when micronutrient levels in the soil are low; so the balance between nutrients and anti-nutritional compounds in the leaves may be an important factor in determining the habitat quality for possums. The carrying capacity of a particular habitat also depends on the availability of subsistence foods when favoured foods are scarce.

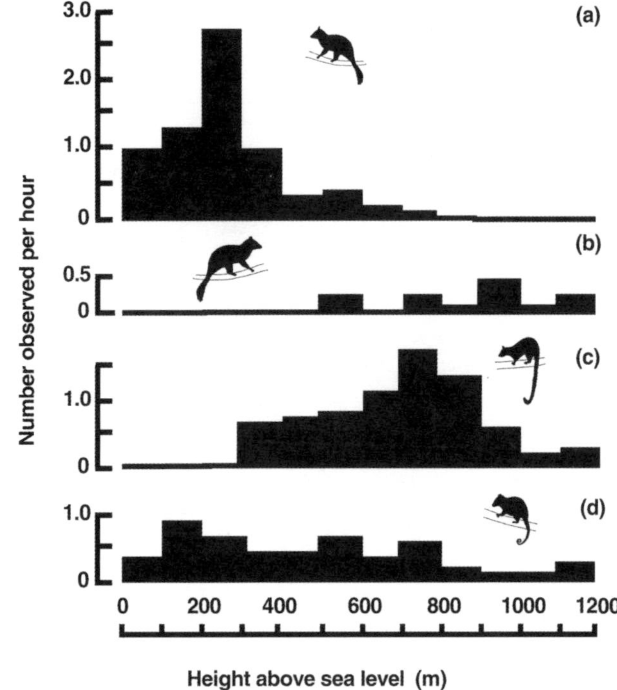

Figure 5.1
These graphs illustrate the variation in abundance of the four possums in relation to height above sea level (from Bennett et al. 1991).
(a) Common Brushtail Possum (b) Mountain Brushtail Possum (c) Greater Glider (d) Common Ringtail Possum.

Forest fires affect the size and maturity of the trees and the density and composition of the shrubby understorey. Mature, nutrient-rich forests with larger trees have more tree hollows suitable for dens and are usually those that have not been burnt very frequently. Possums in southern New South Wales are known to seek flowering trees or those having a flush of new leaf growth as they move around their home range.

In northern Victoria a survey of possums from the high elevation and high rainfall areas of the Dividing Range, through to the dry inland and riverine plains demonstrated differences in habitat preferences between four possum species (Figure 5.1). The Greater Glider and Mountain Brushtail Possum were most abundant in the tall, moist forests of the higher elevations: the Common Brushtail preferred the drier forests and woodlands of the foothills, and the Common Ringtail occurred throughout but at varying densities.

In the more extreme environments of the arid and tropical regions of Australia, water availability is the most important factor influencing possum distribution. In the arid regions, droughts can last for years, resulting in the contraction of populations to small patches of high quality habitat. When conditions improve, the population may be able to build up and disperse temporarily into other areas. In the wet-dry tropics, droughts can be more of an annual event, occurring if there is a poor wet season. This influences the availability of the high quality foods, the condition of the breeding females, and their ability to successfully raise young the following season.

Population density fluctuates in response to the prevailing environmental conditions, and will fluctuate more where the climate is unpredictable. Populations will be more volatile in the arid environment than they are in the temperate forests. Home range size, on the other hand does tend to be stable but there are likely to be seasonal differences in how this area is used.

COMMON BRUSHTAIL POSSUM

The distribution of the Common Brushtail Possum can be divided into eight broadly distinct climatic and geographical regions: the temperate open forests and woodlands of south-eastern Australia (Victoria, South Australia, New South Wales and southern Queensland); Tasmania; arid and semi-arid Australia; tropical open forests and woodlands; tropical rainforests; temperate south-western Western Australia; the urban environment; and the introduced populations in New Zealand.

Hollows in large eucalypts are the usual daytime dens of the Common Brushtail. These may be in the tree trunk or in limb spouts, but possum distribution is not always restricted by the absence of tree hollows. They have been found denning in limestone solution pipes in the ground on Barrow Island, hollows in termite mounds in central Australia, as well as logs, rabbit warrens and rock crevices. In New Zealand they mostly nest above ground in epiphytes (plants growing on other plants, such as ferns on tree trunks) as well as tree hollows but with fewer predators they also readily nest in dense clumps of ground vegetation, in the burrows of other animals or under tree roots and logs. Individuals may use between one and 17 nests within a year but mostly prefer fewer than four.

HABITAT PREFERENCES

In Tasmania they can be found in most of the treed habitats including temperate rainforest, wet and dry sclerophyll forests and woodlands, but not Beech forests. They are rarely found on the large tracts of Buttongrass moorland in the south-west of the island and are most abundant in agricultural areas with a mosaic of pasture and eucalypt forest or woodland. This wide distribution throughout Tasmania appears to be a recent phenomenon. Before 1940 they were confined to forests and mountainous areas but have since increased in abundance and the number of habitats they occupy. Possums of the undisturbed wet forests tend to be larger and have more dark coloured individuals but are less abundant there than in the dry forests. Logging and burning of these forests also affects the population density, with habitat quality being lower in the first few years after fire or logging and most acceptable after 4–6 years.

The dry eucalypt forests, woodlands and timbered watercourses are preferred in temperate south-eastern mainland Australia and while they have been found in sub-alpine woodlands and above the snowline they are generally uncommon in the montane forests of NSW and in the undisturbed tall coastal forests. In these regions Common Brushtails are found in adjoining woodland and regenerating forest. Den trees have a diameter of 55 to 115 centimetres. On Kangaroo Island where they are very common they live in the woodland and dense coastal scrub. They are still common along the Murray River in Victoria and South Australia living in the magnificent River Red Gum forests.

The presence of Mountain Brushtails appears to influence the abundance and distribution of Common Brushtails. At Kioloa north of Batemans Bay where both brushtail species inhabit the Spotted Gum forests, the Common Brushtail was found in the drier forest with a more open understorey than where the Mountain Brushtails were found (Figure 5.2 a, b). Similarly, on the Dorrigo Plateau east of Armidale in NSW, no Common Brushtail Possums were recorded in the closed forest or tall open forest used by the Mountain Brushtail Possums but they were common in the open eucalypt forest grazed woodland and in the grassland.

Figure 5.2

These graphs show the density of the vegetation in forests preferred by each of these possum species and the height above ground level (in metres) where they were most frequently observed (after Davey 1984). (a) Common Brushtail Possum (b) Mountain Brushtail Possum (c) Common Ringtail Possum (d) Greater Glider. (Key: line graph foliage density; bars: % possum sightings)

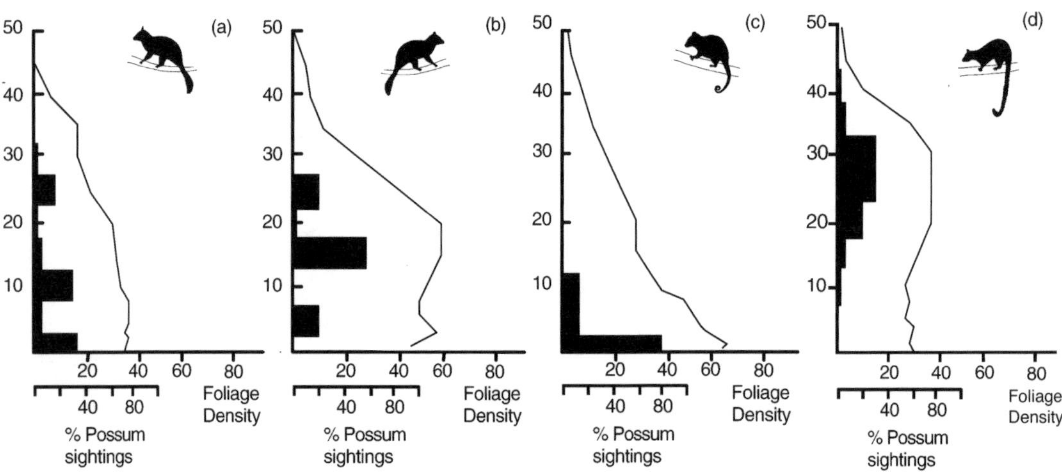

The tropical open forests or woodlands of Woollybut and Stringybark are common and widespread across the north of Australia but the smaller form of the brushtail that occurs there is uncommon, found only in small populations. In the Northern Territory the best indicators of their presence are large Woollybut trees which provide den sites, and a well developed understorey which provides almost all their preferred foods, particularly flowers and fruits (Figure 5.3). They can also be found on the fringes of monsoon forest and rainforest, and feeding in mangroves on the coast.

Figure 5.3 Habitat of the Northern Brushtail Possum near Kakadu, Northern Territory

The Common Brushtail Possum is not found in tropical rainforests except on the western side of the Atherton Uplands between Koombooloomba and Kuranda. There the Coppery Brushtail has its only population, occupying an area of 142 750 hectares. South of there, this habitat is occupied by the Mountain Brushtail Possum and further north these tropical rainforests are the realm of the various large ringtail possums and cuscuses.

There are not many Common Brushtail Possums left in south-west Western Australia but some are found in diverse eucalypt forests and valley woodland. They are not found in the coastal sandplain forest, which is preferred by the sympatric Western Ringtail Possum. Hollows used as dens are found in trees over 30 centimetres diameter and these trees are estimated to be more than 200 years old. Common Brushtails are found also on Barrow Island where, in the absence of large trees, they live in the Spinifex-dominated habitats with a sparse shrubland of figs and wattles.

More than half of the range of the Common Brushtail covers the arid and semi-arid regions of Australia but populations are small and widely separated. The most important places for possums are along rivers, creeks and drainage lines with mature River Red Gums full of hollows (Figure 5.4). Sometimes the density of individuals can be surprisingly high such as on a dry ephemeral billabong in the central west of New South Wales where 11 possums were observed in one hour within a 50-hectare strip of Red Gums (Figure 5.5). The possums use hollows in the gum trees for shelter but feed along the creek line and make forays into the surrounding grassland or shrubland. They can also be found in the mixed eucalypt woodlands of the agricultural regions. In central Australia a few populations remain in the rocky MacDonnell and Petermann ranges (Figure 5.6). If there are no trees with hollows on the rocky hillslopes, they will shelter in cracks and crevices. They have survived in areas having higher levels of surface and ground water and soil nitrogen and a lower frequency of fire than in surrounding areas.

The Common Brushtail has readily adapted to many habitats altered by humans. Residents of Adelaide, Melbourne, Sydney, Brisbane, Canberra, Darwin and many regional centres often consider them a pest. There is plenty of food available of food from fruit trees, decorative garden species and an abundance of scraps, and they are happy to nest in any dark recess, especially in buildings (Figure 5.7). They also use pastures and pine plantations and prosper in areas of farmland in which a few large trees have been left standing. Large numbers of possums have been observed making regular nightly movements from forests to feed in adjacent pasture in Tasmania (with some observations of up to nine possums per hectare), Kangaroo Island and New Zealand. In New Zealand they have colonised the native Podocarp, Rata and mixed hardwood forests in both the North and South Islands.

Figure 5.4
Creeks form important habitat for brushtail possums in central Australia.

Figure 5.5
The Trangie Cowal in central western New South Wales with mature River Red Gums containing hollows.

Figure 5.6
The rocky ranges have become a refuge for brushtails in the arid zone.

Mike Fleming

Figure 5.7 A house-dwelling Common Brushtail Possum.

ABUNDANCE AND HOME RANGE

Estimates of population density and home range size vary from about 4.0 per hectare in Tasmania to 0.2 per hectare elsewhere (Table 5.1). In the tall open forests of Geeveston in Tasmania and Kioloa in New South Wales, the observed variation in population size was related to the structure of the understorey vegetation in the study sites. Patches of high quality habitat can maintain higher possum densities, and individuals can have quite small home ranges as was found in a study in the Northern Territory at Jabiluka (see Table 5.1). As habitat quality decreases and possum densities drop to less than one per hectare, home range size may increase greatly to provide adequate resources. The actual shape of the home range is determined by the distribution of the resources within the habitat.

Apart from Tasmania, Kangaroo Island and urban areas there is evidence of a significant decline in numbers of Common Brushtail Possums, even in the south-east forests. The extensive clearing of open forests and woodlands on the western slopes and tablelands in south-eastern Australia has removed much of their habitat and increasingly people are commenting that the possums are disappearing. Aboriginal information and records from the early European travellers through the arid zone make it clear that these possums were abundant and widespread but in the last sixty or seventy years they have become extremely rare and are found in only a few very small isolated populations. This decline appears to result from the patchiness of suitable habitat, drought, the introduction of rabbits and an increase in predation. In central Australia, population numbers are so low and home range so large that estimates of abundance are extremely difficult to calculate but radio tracking studies by Jeff Foulkes have estimated the minimum home range of one male possum to be about 77 hectares.

Table 5.1
Variation in population size and home range of Common Brushtail Possum populations in Australia in relation to their habitat (After Kerle 1984 & Green 1984).

Location	Site	Possums/ hectare	Home range (hectares)	Habitat description
Kempton Tas		4.0±9.2		Dry sclerophyll forest adjacent to pasture
Beaufort Vic		3.0–3.8		River Red Gum woodland over pasture
Jabiluka NT		3.0±1.5	♂ 1.12±0.5 ♀ 0.89±0.7	Woollybut open forest with diverse understorey
Brisbane Qld		2.1–2.2	♂ 3.71±1.1 ♀ 1.74±0.6	Modified open eucalypt forest; grassy understorey with some shrubs
Geeveston Tas	Site 1	0.23		Tall open eucalypt forest; 1 year since fire
	Site 2	0.79	♂ Appr 9.0 ♀ Appr 6.0	Tall open eucalypt forest; 4–6 years since fire
	Site 3	0.46		Tall open eucalypt forest; 30–40 years since fire
Clouds Creek NSW		0.31–0.44	♂ 7.42±0.71 ♀ 4.67±0.96	Open eucalypt forest and pine plantation
Canberra ACT	Site I/II	0.30	♂ 11.3 ♀ 4.7	Scattered mixed eucalypt woodland over pasture
	Site III	0.39	♂ 6.1 ♀ 4.3	Wooded hill with dense cover of eucalypts & wattles
	Site IV	0.22	♂ 11.1 ♀ 7.4	Semi-natural open eucalypt woodland
	Site V	0.33	♂ 6.1 ♀ 6.1	Semi-natural open eucalypt woodland
	Site VI	0.83	♂ 4.1 ♀ 1.7	Semi-natural scattered eucalypt woodland
	Site VIII	2.35	♂ 1.1 ♀ 0.7	Small isolated patch of natural eucalypts
Kioloa NSW		0.01–0.24		Spotted gum tall forest
Pingelly WA		0.43	♂ 2.55 ♀ 4.62	Valley woodland with Wandoo and casuarina
Launceston Tas			♂ 0.34–42.07 ♀ 0.39–7.01	Urban
Tokoroa New Zealand		0.8–2.4	♂ 1.40±0.37 ♀ 0.93±0.26	2–4 year old pine plantations
New Zealand		8.5	♂ 0.1–3.0 ♀ 0.03–3.8	Podocarp–broadleaf forest
Westland New Zealand		1.9–25.4	♂ 2.5–65.0 ♀ 4.2–45.8	Podocarp–broadleaf forest
New Zealand			♂ 0.5–3.6 ♀ 1.7–4.5	Urban, modified forest

MOUNTAIN BRUSHTAIL POSSUM

The tall wet forests, rainforests, moist gullies and wet sclerophyll forests are the domain of the Mountain Brushtail Possum down the Great Dividing Range and coast of southern Queensland and New South Wales to Spargo Creek in the midlands of Victoria. Their preference for the wetter forests was clearly evident from Ric How's work in northern NSW (Clouds Creek) where they were abundant in the closed forest of Coachwood and Sassafrass tall open forest; common in open forest, peripheral pine plantations and a dense creek association; uncommon in woodland; and absent from the grassland. The density of these possums was 0.42 per hectare in the preferred habitat and 0.28 per hectare in peripheral habitat.

In coastal NSW at Kioloa, Stuart Davey found they preferred the moist forest with a rainforest understorey, which was considerably more dense 10 to 25 metres above the ground, and had many more plant species than the areas occupied by the Common Brushtail Possum (Figure 5.2b). Population density ranged from 0.01 to 0.70 per hectare. Further south in the Coolangubra forest the Mountain Brushtail represented 5 per cent of all arboreal marsupials surveyed, at a density of 0.07 per hectare although this varied across the study area. Most sightings were of animals on the ground (38 per cent) and in wattles and (29 per cent). Only 28 per cent of possums were observed in eucalypt trees, demonstrating the importance of the understorey vegetation. The other major study of the Mountain Brushtail was in the tall eucalypt forests near Cambarville, Victoria by David Lindenmayer where their density ranged from 0.22 to 0.64 per hectare. The number of den trees, a greater density of wattle species and a preference for gullies rather than slopes or ridges were key features of their habitat.

Overall, this species has a restricted habitat preference and individuals show high site fidelity. This suggests that it has a limited ability to survive habitat alteration although their preference for gullies, which are generally left undisturbed, helps with their survival.

Dens used by Mountain Brushtail Possums can be within a few metres of the ground in short, large diameter hollow-bearing trees; trees with multiple hollows not surrounded by dense vegetation; hollow fallen logs or stumps close to the ground; and even wombat burrows. At Cambarville one animal might use up to 23 trees in the course of a year, but mostly they use one to three trees, moving frequently between them. Males and females use different trees and there is very little den sharing, especially between females. This study defined a denning range that overlaps between individuals and tends to be smaller during the breeding season. The denning range is not equivalent to the home range of an animal and the only estimate of home range area is at Clouds Creek where females occupied 5.2±0.6 hectares and males 6.9±0.9 hectares.

COMMON RINGTAIL POSSUM

This possum is primarily a resident of the dense understorey vegetation within the forests of eastern Australia from Cape York to south-eastern South Australia, Tasmania and King, Flinders, Cape Barren and Maria islands. Their habitat includes trees and shrubs which provide their food and an understorey of dense trees, shrubs or tangled growth which the animals can move through without descending to the ground. They are found in habitats from montane forests to temperate rainforest, Antarctic Beech forests, wet and dry sclerophyll forest, woodlands, coastal scrubs and especially along creeks.

The forest understorey can affect the height and abundance of ringtails in the habitat. At Kioloa where they occupy regrowth forest, the majority of animals were observed less than 2.5 metres from the ground within the thickest vegetation (Figure 5.2c). The highest known densities of Common Ringtails have been found in a eucalyptus plantation with a thick shrubby understorey at Lysterfield, southeast of Melbourne where up to 34 ringtails per hectare have been recorded. They are also very abundant (up to 20 per hectare) in the coastal tea-tree scrub at Sandy Point in Port Phillip Bay.

In inland northern Victoria most ringtail possums were observed in the mid stratum and the shrub layer. Further west in northern Victoria they are generally uncommon but can be found in open forests and woodlands where they are usually associated with a tall dense shrub understorey. They also occupy areas without shrubs, nesting in hollows or building dreys in mistletoe. They do not occur in the mallee scrubs of the arid and semi-arid regions.

They are widespread and common in Tasmania, where populations are most abundant in the wet scrub and tea-tree thickets along creeks. They are also scattered through the wet and dry eucalypt forests and agricultural areas. Tasmanian Ringtails were apparently more abundant before 1940. At that time populations suddenly dropped and continued to decline significantly over the ensuing fifteen years. Populations have since recovered but not to the pre-1940 levels.

In north-eastern NSW they are more common in cool and cold montane forests, in rainforest and in rainforest-like communities in gullies and creeks traversing the eucalypt woodlands of the Richmond and Clarence River catchments. They are not found in tropical rainforests except at the southern end of the Cooktown–Townsville rainforest block. On Cape York their distribution within the open forests and woodlands is very patchy and there are concerns that these populations are disappearing.

Common Ringtails are well established and often quite abundant in the urban environment. Like the brushtail they enjoy eating many of the planted tree species but because they are entirely vegetarian they may rely on creek habitats to provide suitable food supplements. They also seem to be able to survive some disturbance to their natural habitat and readily recolonise regenerating forest after logging. They do not inhabit pine plantations although they may live in some native vegetation remnants within the plantations. They do not respond well to forest thinning, which removes their preferred dense understorey.

Because Common Ringtail Possums are skilled nest builders they are not restricted to forests with suitable hollow bearing trees like other possum species. In some areas tree hollows are preferred and in the north of their range dreys are seldom built. When dens are preferred an individual may use up to five den trees and the hollows are variable in size. In a study of ringtails released into Kuringai Chase National Park, 21 per cent remained in the artificial dreys where they had been released, 46 per cent constructed their own dreys, 25 per cent used tree hollows and 8 per cent were in ground nests. Females used more tree hollows than males. During extremely hot conditions dreys may not provide enough insulation as indicated by many deaths in one population of Ringtail Possums studied by Lester Pahl during a very hot summer in Victoria.

Dreys (Figure 5.8) are constructed in a shrub or tree fork within dense vegetation, mistletoes, accumulated debris caught in trees, loose bark, stumps and hollow logs. Leaves, twigs, fronds or grasses are woven tightly together for the outer structure and lined with fine bark or twigs, ferns, moss or grass. The dreys are generally spherical, 25 to 30 centimetres in diameter on the outside with an entrance hole 8 to 10 centimetres across. The hole is usually in line with a trunk or branch that the animals use as a runway. Bundles of building materials are carried in the coiled tail.

Figure 5.8 Ringtail Possum drey

Home range size has been determined for only a few Common Ringtail Possum populations. If there is a very high density of possums and the habitat area is quite small, there is a high degree of sharing with other possums. This was the case at Sandy Point where the home range was only 0.33 hectares. At Lysterfield, home range estimates were 2.6 hectares for males, 2.1 hectares for females but in the Warramate Hills with a population density of 2.4 to 3.5 per hectare, they occupied an area only 15 metres in diameter. They live in groups of up to five animals and share nests.

WESTERN RINGTAIL POSSUM

The Western Ringtail Possum is found on the coastal plain from the Harvey River to areas east of Albany and there are only a few inland populations: at Collie, Perup, Manjimup and the Porongurup National Park. Even though it is a rare species, it can be locally common as it is at Perup, and some populations have adapted to the urban environment.

Western Australian Peppermint trees (which are not eucalypts) are always present in the coastal habitats occupied by Western Ringtails including the urban populations. Western Ringtails are also associated with creeks, swamps, rivers, and drainage channels or live less than two kilometres from the sea. They once occupied a wider range of forest types — eucalypt forests with Marri, Jarrah and Blackbutt — many of which did not include the Peppermint tree, especially in inland areas. In the coastal populations studied by Barbara Jones, population density varied from 0.1 to 4.5 possums per hectare, and at Perup it is possible to observe 16 ringtails in two hours of spotlighting from a slowly moving vehicle.

The level of nitrogen in the leaves of the preferred food plants is a key factor determining the distribution of the Western Ringtail. They also require a high degree of canopy or understorey continuity — places with lush, dense vegetation — and trees with hollows. The latter are not widely available in the coastal Peppermint forest where the ringtails build dreys; however, dreys are uncommon in the inland forests where hollows are preferred, perhaps for sheltering from high daytime temperatures.

GREATER GLIDER

The Greater Glider resides in the tall eucalypt forests from north of Cairns, south through eastern NSW to the eastern half of Victoria and is more abundant in the wetter eucalypt forests at higher elevations. In the Paluma Range north west of Townsville the smaller northern Greater Gliders are common in mature eucalypt forests.

Their distribution throughout these forests is patchy. The most important characteristic of the habitat appears to be the level of nutrients in eucalypt leaves, their favoured food. Near Eden they were absent or occurred only at very low densities where leaf nitrogen fell below 1.1 g%

and were at higher densities if the nitrogen levels were 1.1–1.6 g%. The higher nutrients levels are found in Peppermint (eucalypt) forests. In north-eastern Victoria 44 per cent of observations were in Peppermint and at Coolangubra the preferred trees were Peppermint (24 per cent of sightings), Manna Gum (29 per cent) and Brown Barrel (21 per cent). These percentages differ significantly from the actual proportions of these tree species in the forest. In addition, tree preference varied throughout the year with Peppermint being most important in winter and Manna Gum when it has new leaf growth in spring. The Greater Glider generally feeds high in the canopy with most sightings at Kioloa being 25–30 metres above the ground (Figure 5.2d).

The availability of high hollows in large old large trees is another critical component of Greater Glider habitat. An individual glider may use 2 to 18 dens, which are generally entered through hollow branches and can be in either dead or living trees. In a south-eastern Queensland study, nest hollows were about 10 metres above the ground, the diameter of the entrance hole was 18 centimetres and the minimum tree size was 54 centimetres diameter. In Mountain Ash at Cambarville the hollows are mostly 40 metres above the ground and experimental evidence from nest boxes indicates that the gliders prefer deep hollows. Nest construction in the den appears to be minimal but rudimentary nests have been found both in the wild and in captivity.

The easily spotlighted Greater Glider rarely comes to the forest floor so population size is mostly determined from spotlighting surveys along roads where it is often the most frequently recorded arboreal species. In the high elevation forest near Queanbeyan Greater Gliders were 87 per cent of all possum sightings, and 62 per cent of all sightings at Coolangubra and 40 per cent near Eden, but this may not reflect the relative densities of the possum species. Greater Glider densities range from 0.01 per hectare in parts of the Kioloa forest to 5.5 per hectare in north-eastern NSW but density is mostly less than one glider per hectare. Their home range size varies from about 2.5 hectares in south-east Queensland to 1.3–4.4 hectares (males) and 0.9–1.7 hectares (females) near Townsville, 1.5–2 hectares (males) and 1.4 hectares (females) in south east NSW and 1.4–2 hectares (males) and 1.3 hectares (females) in Gippsland.

The need for specific types of hollows and the restricted gum leaf diet of Greater Gliders probably explain their inability to survive clearing of their habitat. Near Queanbeyan the numbers of Greater Gliders were twice as high in unlogged moist forest than in logged compartments and they have not colonised pine forests.

CHAPTER 6

FOOD AND NUTRITION

THE PROBLEM OF BEING A SMALL ARBOREAL FOLIVORE

It seems easy for a herbivore to feed, just by sitting on a branch and chewing the surrounding leaves. A carnivore however has to chase and catch its prey. But do herbivores have such an easy life? Once a carnivore has caught its prey, it has a high-protein meal rich in water, vitamins and minerals, with variable fat content (depending on the prey) but low levels of carbohydrates. Muscle and intestines are highly digestible and the predator's glucose and energy requirements are readily obtained from amino acids. Plant foods contain highly digestible lipids, sugars, starches, soluble proteins, vitamins and amino acids but these are all locked inside little boxes, the cell walls. These are made from the structural carbohydrates cellulose and hemicellulose as well as lignin, and are often referred to as fibre. In order to obtain its nutrition, a herbivore has to crack the cell walls to gain access to the cell contents and to digest the cell walls themselves to supply the carbohydrate. The nutritional value of plant foods varies with the proportion of cell wall to cell content. Added to this, plants vary substantially in availability and quality and they really don't want to be eaten so they have developed a range of anti-herbivore defence strategies that include some nasty chemical and physical deterrents. Plants are in fact quite a hostile food source!

Herbivores have developed ways of overcoming these problems to obtain sufficient nutrition and energy. Cell walls are broken down or digested in several ways: mechanically, by chewing and grinding; chemically, by digestive juices, and biologically, by a variety of bacteria and other gut microbes. The anatomy of the herbivore's gut varies too, with some herbivores fermenting the food in the foregut and others using the hindgut. Many herbivores have a low basal metabolic rate (see Chapter 3) and spend a lot of time just sitting, conserving their energy and reducing their food needs. In addition, possums generally have a low nitrogen requirement, low water turnover, and a concentrated urine, which together reduce their need for water.

There are also dietary constraints for possums because of their size. Most mammal species that live on fibrous plant tissue are large: horses, cattle, giraffes, elephants and antelopes. This is partly a result of the physical limit (that is, the gut capacity) to the amount of cell wall that can be processed in the digestive tract. The ruminants (for example cows) are an extreme example of this, having greatly enlarged forestomachs where the fibrous food particles are fermented and reduced to the required size. The total capacity of the digestive tract and the amount of microbial fermentation that can occur is in proportion to the body weight of the animal.

The energy requirement of a herbivore is also related to body size: the total energy intake required per day is directly in proportion to body weight:

$$\text{total daily energy consumption } \alpha \text{ (body mass)}^{0.75}$$

Studies of the physiology of mammals and their energy needs suggest that possums are too small to be able to survive on a diet of leaves alone. They are closer to their digestive and metabolic limits than most other herbivores.

In order to balance the amount of energy required to extract nutrients from their food and the energy required for survival and reproduction, possums either use special strategies to extract more from their uncooperative food source or vary their diet. Because they are small, possums need to avoid the highly fibrous parts of plants and instead select foods that are high in available energy such as young leaves, flowers, fruits, buds and seeds. Alternatively they have evolved special digestive or metabolic mechanisms to overcome the problems they face. It has been suggested that Greater Gliders cope with the low nutritional value of gum leaves because they have a low metabolic rate, and low levels of activity, and gliding is an energy-efficient way of moving around.

Food selection plays an important role in the feeding strategies of herbivores. Eucalypts are the most common trees in the Australian forests and woodlands, yet their leaves are an important food source for only four mammal species: the Greater Glider, Common Ringtail Possum, Common Brushtail Possum and the Koala. Eucalypt leaves are not a very valuable food resource: they have a low concentration of nutrients, are very fibrous and contain unpalatable chemicals called antifeedants or antinutrients. In some places leaves from only one or two trees of a species will be eaten while others are ignored. In addition to being specific in their plant food choices, many mammal species cannot be strictly defined as herbivores because they supplement their energy supply, either regularly or seasonally, with animal food.

In summary, these small folivores have three basic strategies for obtaining sufficient nutrition and energy from their food (explored further in the next section):

- physical adaptation of the teeth and the gut to effectively break down the fibre;
- development of metabolic processes for energy conservation and detoxification of the food; and
- behavioural mechanisms such as choosing very specific foods and reducing their energy needs.

EXTRACTING NOURISHMENT: THE TEETH AND GUT

The teeth

The size and structure of the teeth of an animal are a good indicator of its preferred food: sharp tearing teeth for tearing meat and flat grinding teeth for crushing plant cell walls. For a herbivore, chewing is essential for breaking the cell walls, releasing the cell contents and then reducing the cell walls to the smallest possible particle size to assist the fermentation process.

As already discussed these possums are diprotodonts, marsupials with cutting incisors at the front of the mouth, generally very small canine teeth and a large gap (diastema) in front of the flat grinding molar tooth row at the back. All possums in the Phalangeridae and the Pseudocheiridae are herbivorous and have this basic tooth form but there are some differences that reflect variation in their food preferences. The molars are flat and designed for grinding food but the shape of the bumps (cusps) on the biting (occlusal) surface differs (Figure 6.1). Brushtail and cuscus molars have cusps partially connected by ridges (sub-lophodont form) while the cusps on ringtail molars are crescent shaped and the molar row is more elongated (selenodont form) (see Figure 3.3). The crescent shape creates a series of scissor-like triangles that grind leaves into very fine particles in preparation for bacterial fermentation of the fibre in the gut. With age the cusps wear down, the efficiency of grinding decreases, particle size increases and the cell contents are not all released.

(a)

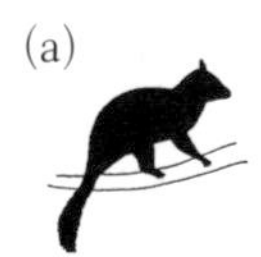

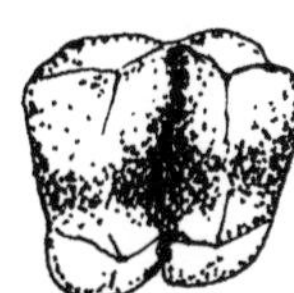

(b)

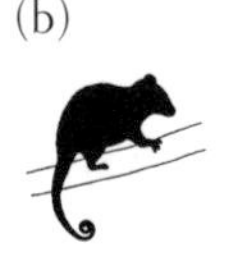

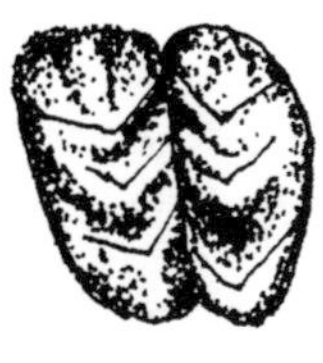

Figure 6.1 The upper molar of (a) the Common Brushtail Possum showing the four pointed cusps and (b) the Common Ringtail which has crescent shaped ridges.

There are differences also in the size and shape of the canine and premolar teeth. The brushtail possums and cuscuses have larger canines than the ringtail possums and Greater Glider. In the Phalangeridae the first upper premolar is like a small canine tooth and the third premolar has a high crown, is conical or blade-shaped and set at an angle to the molar row. It is more of a cutting tooth than the third premolar of the ringtail possums, which forms a part of the grinding tooth row and has two or three cusps.

The digestive tract

The digestive tract of herbivores is greatly enlarged and specialised when compared with non-herbivorous species. Its volume is greater so that the passage of food can be delayed to provide both more time for microbial fermentation and a larger surface area for the absorption of the digested foods. The length, volume and surface area of the gut increases with the importance of leaves in the diet. The size and structure of the gut also differs between brushtails, ringtails and Greater Gliders. These differences reflect their food preferences as well as the different ways they digest their food.

Fermentation of the ground food particles by herbivores can take place in the hindgut or the foregut; kangaroos are foregut fermenters and possums have hindgut fermentation. Hindgut fermentation can also be divided into two types: fermentation in which there is no separation of the large and small food particles in the colon; and fermentation in which the caecum is the primary site for microbial activity and there is selective retention of small particles within the caecum. The stomachs of species that ferment their food in the hindgut have a simple structure when compared with the foregut fermenters such as kangaroos.

The Common Brushtail Possum has a well-developed caecum and proximal colon (Figure 6.2) that work together as a single fermentation chamber. Different sized particles do not move at different rates through the gut — they do not selectively retain any of the particles for extra fermentation. The rate of passage of particles through the gut is determined by the amount of fibre present. In brushtails the rate of passage is slower than in sheep and kangaroos: in one experiment fluids took 66 hours to pass through and coarse particles 71 hours but this varies with the food type.

In the ringtail possums and Greater Glider there is more specialisation for leaf fermentation with a greatly enlarged and complex caecum (Figures 6.3 and 6.4) as well as a special mechanism for controlling the flow of particles between the caecum and the colon. The caecum is more complex in structure than for the Common Brushtail Possum, with the muscles in the walls being arranged in longitudinal bands (taeniae) with little sac like structures in between. This shape, in association with contraction of the wall muscles, helps mix the food particles. Symbiotic bacteria in the caecum assist in breaking down the food particles. Not all ringtail possum species have the same gut structure — the Green Ringtail, for example, has a smaller caecum and a particularly large colon and the Herbert River Ringtail has a very large caecum.

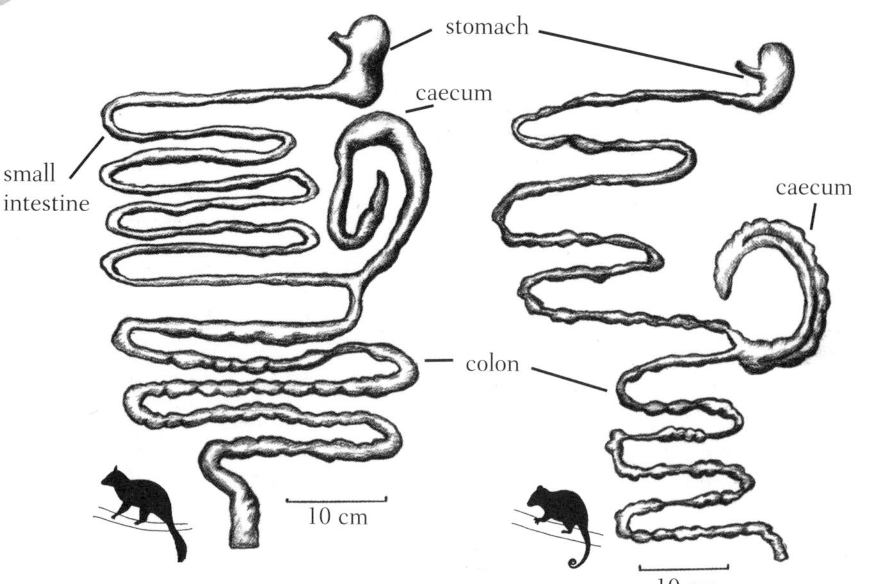

Figure 6.2 (far left) The digestive tract of the Common Brushtail Possum (drawn from Hume 1999).

Figure 6.3 (left) The digestive tract of the Common Ringtail Possum (drawn from Hume 1999).

As in brushtail possums, the passage of food particles and fluids through the gut is slow. In studies of Common Ringtail Possums eating eucalypt leaves, markers of coarse particles took 63 hours, and fluids and small particles took 35 hours, to pass through the digestive tract. In both common ringtails and Greater Gliders coarse particles pass through the gut in about half the time it takes for fluids and fine particles — they selectively retain parts of their food within the gut for further digestion. Separation of the different sized food particles occurs in the proximal colon with the small particles being washed into the caecum while the large particles continue their passage through the colon. These mammals survive on a highly fibrous diet by retaining the most nutritious portion and minimising the loss of nitrogen in the faeces.

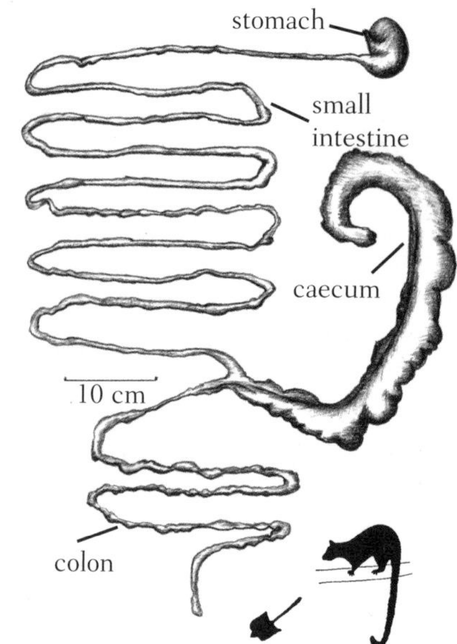

The process of selective retention is thought to be a response to the high fibre content of eucalypt leaves and the difficulty of extracting sufficient nutrients. It also provides a mechanism to explain how Greater Gliders and common ringtails can survive entirely on eucalyptus leaves while brushtail possums need a more varied diet. In addition, the Greater Glider and Common Ringtail Possum obtain only 8–16 per cent of their daily energy needs from the fermentation of the complex cell-wall sugars of gum leaves; this mostly comes from the simple carbohydrates, proteins and lipids in the cell contents.

Figure 6.4 (above) The digestive tract of the Greater Glider (drawn from Hume 1999).

The Common Ringtail Possum has gone even further with specific adaptations. It is particularly efficient at recycling urea and then using this for the production of microbial protein in the hindgut. The gut microbes enable them to digest a relatively high proportion of the fibre from gum leaves. Common ringtails also eat some of their faeces, a behaviour called coprophagy. They produce two types of faeces: larger soft faeces which are moist, have a smooth texture and are partially excreted during daylight (non-foraging) hours and hard faeces produced during the active night-time period. The contents of the caecum are excreted after fermentation as the soft faeces and the possum eats these immediately. As this passes through the gut for the second time, more nutrients are absorbed and the resultant waste material becomes the fully digested hard pellets. Because ringtail possums consume the soft faeces so efficiently, it was not until experiments conducted in 1983 that their existence was confirmed although it had been suspected for some time. Green Ringtails, which feed extensively on very fibrous mature fig leaves, also practice coprophagy.

Coping with anti-herbivore toxins and chemicals

Plants have evolved many mechanisms for deterring herbivores from eating them. These range from structures like prickles and spikes to chemicals such as naturally occurring sodium monofluoracetate, which is more commonly known as the poison 1080. Leaf chemistry, its influence on food selection, and the nutritional quality of selected possum foods have been studied in some detail, but the focus has been on the compounds commonly found in eucalypt leaves: phenolics (including tannins) and terpenes. Despite this focus, the ways in which possums overcome the defences of eucalypt trees is still not clear and there is a need to examine their tolerance to other plant poisons like the monofluoroacetates and alkaloids.

Eucalypt antifeedants

It is difficult for a possum to survive on a diet of eucalypt leaves, which generally have low levels of minerals, protein and available carbohydrates and an abundance of antifeedant compounds. Antifeedants work in one of two ways: by interfering with the digestive process or by having a direct toxic effect on the animal. Lignin and tannins are compounds that interfere with the digestive process while other phenolic compounds and the essential oils are known to be toxic.

Eucalyptus leaves contain a diverse range of phenolic compounds. The presence of lignin in the cell walls reduces the digestibility of gum leaves while tannins can bind with the protein molecules and reduce the available protein. These indicate that there are metabolic costs associated with the consumption of these compounds but there is no strong evidence demonstrating that they significantly affect the survival of a possum. The specialised folivores including Greater Gliders and ringtail possums seem to be able to overcome the effects of tannins in gum leaves. The tannin-protein complexes are broken down in the caecum and this probably counteracts the antifeedant impact of the tannin molecules. The colon-fermenting brushtail possums would be more affected by tannins if they relied entirely on a diet of gum leaves.

The very distinctive essential oils found in eucalypt leaves are known as terpenes. Higher concentrations of these aromatic compounds (the eucalypt smell) have been thought to deter arboreal folivores especially as they can be toxic to the gut microbes that are so important for the digestion of the plant cell walls. Observations that possums and Koalas smell leaves before eating or rejecting them has suggested that high levels of terpenes are not acceptable but results of studies of the importance of this factor have been confusing. Koalas, for example, prefer eucalypt species with higher concentrations! Terpenes are mostly absorbed and digested in the foregut so the impact of these compounds should be minimal for the hindgut fermenting possum species.

Recent studies have found yet another group of antifeedant compounds that commonly occur in eucalypt leaves. These are called FPCs (formylphloroglucinol compounds) and have a structure similar to both phenols and terpenes. Variation in the concentration of these compounds in leaves seems to explain much of the variation shown by Common Ringtail Possums in eucalypt leaf choice experiments. This may explain their preference for one individual tree over an adjacent tree of the same species. As yet we do not understand the effect of these compounds on an animal. FPCs appear to have no smell or taste but there is some evidence that the animals use the smell of the terpenes as an indicator for the presence of FPCs.

Other compounds

Alkaloids are toxic compounds that are uncommon in eucalypt leaves but are found in some other possum food species. The Ironwood tree (*Erythrophleum chlorostachys*) is common in the open forests of the tropical north of Australia. Its leaves, while containing an extremely toxic and lethal alkaloid for sheep, cattle and camels, can form a major component of the diet of the Northern Brushtail Possum and are also eaten by the Rock Ringtail Possum. As yet there has been no study into how possums survive when consuming Ironwood leaves while cattle cannot. In Queensland, Common Brushtail Possums also eat *Solanum mauritianum*, another species with a high concentration of alkaloids.

Sodium monofluoracetate is generally highly toxic to mammals and widely used to poison pests such as foxes, feral cats and wild dogs. After an animal eats this poison it is converted to fluorocitrate causing citrate accumulation, which affects the ability to metabolise food. Despite its known toxicity, not all mammals are equally susceptible to the effect of 1080 and in Western Australia, several native mammal species, including the Common Brushtail Possum, are unusually tolerant. Results of trials of the tolerance of brushtail possums to the 1080 poison are dramatic: the Western Australian individuals can tolerate 1080 at a concentration more than one hundred times greater than possums from New South Wales.

Many plant species in the genera *Gastrolobium* and *Oxylobium* found in Western Australia naturally contain high levels of monofluoracetate. These toxic plants are highly nutritious legumes that respond rapidly after fire and undoubtedly represent an important food source in this nutrient-poor environment. Tolerant animals are better able to break down the toxic fluorocitrate molecule but this ability is limited and these plants could provide only about one third of the daily food intake. There is no information about the food eaten by possums in these parts of Western Australia but it seems most probable that these toxic plants and the tolerant herbivores have evolved together.

Food choice

Food choice is the third way a possum can ensure that it will obtain sufficient nutrition and energy, avoiding the poorest quality plant foods and selecting shoots, fruits and flowers in preference. Unfortunately none of these represent the ideal food supply and it is a constant challenge for possums to obtain enough of that most important nutrient, protein. Eucalypt leaves are low in protein and plant defences tend to make the protein less available. Fruits are also low in available protein and may contain antifeedants (tannins, terpenes, anthocyanidins and alkaloids) but generally they contain more readily digestible carbohydrates (sugars and starch) than leaves. Except for fruits with fibrous pods they also have a lower concentration of fibre (cell walls). Possums must balance all these factors when deciding which food to eat and when. Observations of the feeding behaviour of several possum species have indicated that they can be very specific in their selection of foods. For example, the Herbert River Ringtail Possum specifically selects leaves containing significantly higher levels of protein.

The food preferences of each possum species have been studied by two methods:

- observing animals while they are feeding, noting which plant species and parts of the plant are eaten as well as the amount of time spent feeding on a particular food; or
- by analysing the plant fragments found in their faeces.

This information is very important when trying to understand why a species selects a particular habitat to live in, especially when determining the conservation needs of the species.

Common Brushtail Possum

The Common Brushtail Possum is very flexible in its food choices with food preferences varying substantially between habitats (Table 6.1). The most common plants are not necessarily their preferred foods.

Table 6.1 Variation in the diet of the Common Brushtail Possum

Location & year of study	Eucalypt leaf (%)	Other leaf species (%)
Near Hobart (Tas) Site 1, 1984	7	40 Beech tree 14 Mosses, ferns 20 Other
Near Hobart (Tas) Site 2, 1984	Approx 10	20 Wattle 20 Pommaderris 20 ferns
Kempton, south-east, Tas, 1984	18	20 Wattle Fern
Beaufort, central Victoria, 1983	95	0
Victoria & NSW, 1964	72	4.5 Wattle
Kangaroo Island, SA, 1964	0	100 Tea tree & pea bushes
Brisbane, Qld, 1975	66	4 fig, other trees Ipomoea
Townsville, McKay Qld, 1964	80	20 Adenanthera Melaleuca
Eungella & Atherton Qld, 1964	0	91 Alphitonia
Atherton, Qld, 1982	0	53
Weipa, N Qld, 1984	2–8	63 Ironwood 4 Vines
Jabiluka, NT, 1984	3.5	7 Ironwood 24 other shrubs
Magela Point, NT 1984	3	54 Ironwood 6 other shrubs
Kapalga, NT, 1984	5	40 Ironwood 5 other shrubs
Nourlangie, NT, 1984	47	20 Understorey shrubs
Pingelly, south west WA, 1980	50	She-oak
Busselton, south west WA, 1999	1–51	45–84 Peppermint tree 17 Radiata pine
Irving Ck, central Australia, NT, 1998	14–24	13–22 Wattles 27–52 other shrubs
Loves Ck, central Australia, NT, 1998	6	2–11 Wattles 18–56 other shrubs
Central Australia, NT, 1986	<3	9–23 Wattles 11–50 other shrubs

Grasses or herbs (%)	Flowers & fruits (%)	Insects	Habitat type
10 - 20	Trace	—	Wet sclerophyll forest, selectively logged
20 Herbs 20 grasses	Trace	—	Wet sclerophyll forest, logged, burnt & resown
13 Forest 22–60Pasture	Significant proportions	—	Dry sclerophyll forests and adjacent pasture
5–80	—	1–5 January only	Open eucalypt woodland, farmland
23.5	—	—	Dry sclerophyll forest
—	—	—	Low coastal scrub
23	7	2 obs	Slightly disturbed open forest, grassy understorey
—	—	—	Savannah woodland
9	—	—	Tropical rainforest
2	45	—	Tropical rainforest
—	17	—	Stringybark open forest
Trace	59	present	Woollybut open forest
Trace	38	present	Mature mixed open forest
0	50	Present	Woollybut open forest
0	38	Trace	Monsoon forest / open eucalypt forest
—	—	—	Eucalypt woodland
—	—	—	Swamp Gum & Tuart woodland Pine plantation & gums
< 1	19–52 seasonal variation	2–5.5	River Red Gum creekline surrounded by arid shrubland
< 1–2	20–58 seasonal variation	2–5	Steep rocky hills with wattles and other shrubs and trees
< 3	39	<1	Arid shrublands and creek woodland

Eucalyptus leaves vary from being absent or very uncommon in the diet of tropical rainforest Common Brushtails, to less than 10 per cent of the food of animals in the Tasmanian wet sclerophyll forests, the open forests of the wet–dry tropics. In the eucalypt forests of south-eastern Australia the proportion of leaves in the diet ranges from 66 per cent in an area with a variety of shrub species to 95 per cent in a habitat with scattered eucalypts over pasture. The proportion of grasses and herbs, leaves of other species, flowers and fruits also varies between the habitats.

The use of supplementary foods such as flowers and fruits has been recorded regularly in the brushtail diet. In the Woollybut open forests of tropical Australia, leaves of the Ironwood tree are the most common food in addition to a large proportion of flowers and fruits. Where the Ironwood was uncommon, it was mostly replaced by more flowers and fruits. In central Australia where the supply of food resources is unreliable they have a varied diet with 32 food items being recorded. The consumption of these items changes through time and between populations. In this study, Jeff Foulkes found that possums preferentially selected wattle flowers and the leaves of plumbush and mistletoes even when these were uncommon in the habitat. The possums also opportunistically ate some ephemeral herb species in large quantities. Supplementary foods are less important in temperate Australia.

The importance of insects and meat in the diet of the Common Brushtail Possum is difficult to assess. There are numerous records of captive possums actively preying on birds and insects and although insect remains have been found in diet analyses it is often difficult to determine whether they were actively or accidentally consumed. The presence of large quantities of caterpillars in the stomachs of possums in New Zealand as found by Mick Clout and up to 5 per cent in the summer diet of some Victorian Common Brushtail Possums provide evidence that they will utilise these foods as necessary. Beetles and grasshopper remains have been recorded in their diet in central Australia and there are observations in New Zealand of possums actively searching for fly larvae in the leaf litter and congregating around lights to catch large moths.

In New Zealand Common Brushtail Possums eat mostly leaves but flowers and fruits are also important and can provide 40 per cent of their diet. More than 70 tree species, 20 ferns, some vines, grasses, forbs and sedges are known possum foods but there are a few preferred species and these vary between the habitats occupied by possums. They have definite preferences when they first colonise an area and then change their preferences as the original favourites are eaten out. They are also seasonally opportunistic, often travelling long distances to feed. Their preference for some flowers and fruits can cause considerable damage and is affecting the survival of some indigenous fruit-eating bird species.

Mountain Brushtail Possum

The Mountain Brushtail Possum is considered to be a wholly herbivorous species although there have been a few observations of insect remains in the faeces, and captive animals have eagerly eaten cooked meat when provided. It obtains most of its food from plant species in the understorey or on the ground: leaves of shrubs, fruits, buds, fungi, lichens and bark, and about 25 per cent of the available plant species are eaten regularly.

At Cambarville in Victoria the leaves of the Silver Wattle were strongly preferred over all other foods throughout the year. Fungi were the second most common food and although they are seasonal in their occurrence possums seek them out at almost all times of the year. Ten types of fungi have been identified in their diets with eight of these being underground-fruiting types. This may indicate that Mountain Brushtail Possums assist in the spread of fungi that play an important role in plant nutrition. Tree ferns, Victorian Christmas Bush, Blackberry, Bidgee-widgee, Myrtle Beech, Montane Wattle and Hazel Pommaderris were eaten seasonally, and flowers, seeds and fruits were important in late spring and early summer. They do not eat Mountain Ash, the dominant plant species in their habitat.

Mountain Brushtail Possums are also known to remove the bark from around the base of the trunk of young pine trees and eat the growing tissue from underneath, and to attack the upper parts of the trees, causing straggly lateral growth. While male pine cones were eaten almost to the exclusion of other foods in winter and early spring in one study, pine needles have been recorded only infrequently in their diets.

Common and Western Ringtail Possums

These two possum species are entirely herbivorous and mostly folivorous, much more so than would be predicted by their small size. At Sandy Point in southern Victoria Lester Pahl found that eucalypt leaves made up 61–98 per cent of the diet. They preferred to eat young leaves when they were available, mainly in spring and summer, providing 5 to 45 per cent of the diet. Mistletoe leaves are another food source. Leaves of some understorey plants were eaten and these were a more important component of the diet when the preferred eucalypt species were less abundant, such as in the coastal tea tree thickets. The use of understorey species as a supplementary food is also more significant in areas with high population densities such as at Sandy Point where leaves of the Prickly Tea Tree were eaten. Flowers and fruits do not appear to be important but may be eaten at times. An individual usually feeds only on one or two species each night.

While none of the diet studies have any evidence that ringtail possums eat insect foods, there have been persistent suggestions that they will take eggs. There is circumstantial evidence of ringtails taking Lyrebird eggs with observations that any Lyrebird nests built within 10 metres of a ringtail drey lost the egg within a week of it being laid, and a ringtail has been disturbed in a Lyrebird nest two metres from its drey.

The Western Ringtail Possum also has limited food preferences. In habitats near Abba in coastal south-west Western Australia, leaves of the Peppermint (*Agonis flexuosa*) made up 79 to 100 per cent of the diet. In the inland habitat at Perup they ate mostly leaves of the two eucalypt species, Marri and Jarrah. Unlike the Common Brushtail Possum in south-west western Australia, the Ringtail Possum has not developed a tolerance to fluoroacetate (the toxic compound found in some understorey species and in the poison 1080), supporting the evidence that these species are not important in the diet of the Western Ringtail.

Greater Glider

The Greater Glider feeds almost exclusively on eucalypt leaves. Young leaves are preferentially eaten when they are present and the gliders favour individual trees with most new growth. Buds are also eaten commonly when available, mainly in winter and spring when young leaves are not available. Eucalypt flowers are rarely eaten. Mistletoe, *Allocasuarina, Melaleuca* and *Pommaderris* are the only non-eucalypt foods that have been recorded in the Greater Glider diet.

In the Coolangubra Forest of south-east NSW they prefer the young leaves of the Manna Gum (*E. viminalis*), which have the highest ratio of nitrogen to fibre of all the species there. Brown Barrel (*E. fastigata*), Narrow-leaved Peppermint (*E. radiata*) and White Stringybark (*E. globoidea*) are also important species as are the buds of the Swamp Gum (*E. ovata*). In north-east Queensland they eat the same food types and have a preference for the White Mahogany (*E. acmenoides*).

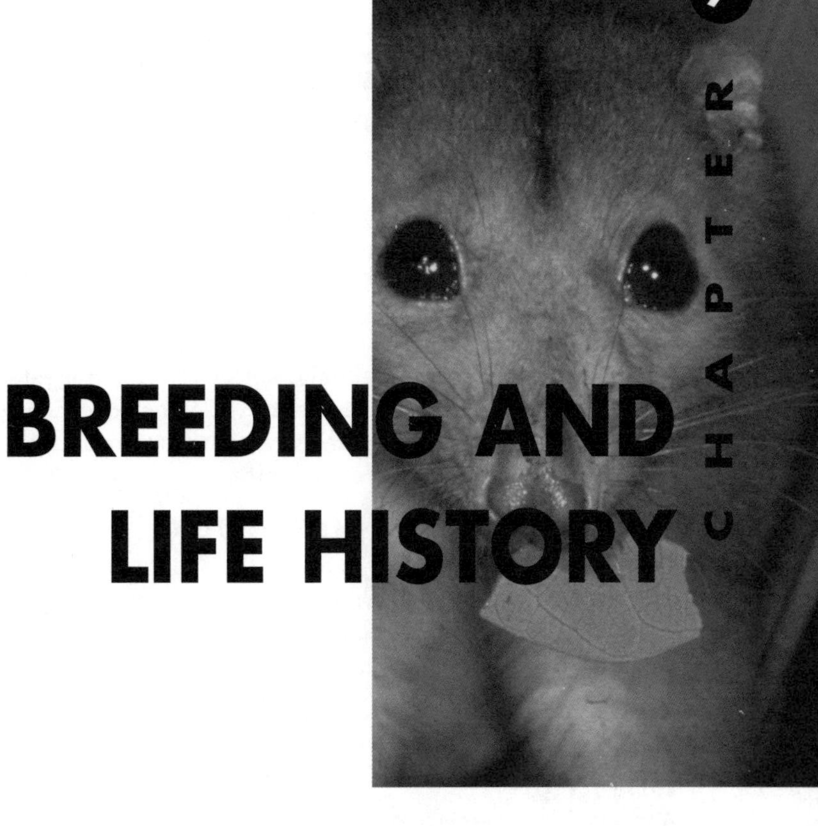

BREEDING AND LIFE HISTORY

The breeding cycle and life history strategies of each species are largely determined by the species size and physiology, and by climatic conditions, habitat type and food quality. The life history strategies of the ringtail and brushtail possums differ distinctly (see Table 7.1) as do their habitat preferences and diet, although most young are born at a time that allows them to leave the pouch when their food is most available and nutritious. The timing of breeding, litter size, number of litters per year, rate of growth and development, survival of the young and the age at first breeding can all vary to enable the species to successfully reproduce and survive.

When all reproductive factors are considered in association with climatic and habitat constraints, the reproductive strategies of these species fall into a fast–slow continuum. The Common Brushtail Possum and the Common Ringtail Possum are capable of more rapid rates of population growth because they mature earlier and are capable of producing more young per year than the other species. The Common Brushtail has an especially flexible life history strategy that is influenced by the suitability and carrying capacity of the various habitats they occupy across Australia and in New Zealand. Populations are readily able to colonise or recolonise disturbed habitat by altering fecundity, behaviour and diet, and can recover from periods of unfavourable conditions in the less favourable parts of their range. The Greater Glider and Mountain Brushtail Possum are towards the slower end of the range of strategies. These two species occupy vegetation communities that are naturally quite stable. In these habitats the Mountain Brushtail populations are self-regulated by mortality and reduced fecundity and can out-compete the Common Brushtail Possum.

REPRODUCTIVE SYSTEM

The birth of a tiny unfurred baby, which crawls into a pouch where it stays for a long time suckling and growing, is the best-known feature distinguishing a marsupial from other mammals. But the differences between marsupial and placental breeding biology are much greater than this: the internal arrangement of the reproductive organs in both males and females, the structure of the egg, the process of fertilisation, and the method of sustaining the young in the uterus all differ.

THE FEMALE REPRODUCTIVE SYSTEM

The female reproductive system of the Common Brushtail Possum has been studied in more detail than for any other possum but there do appear to be some features in common between this species and the other large possums. Like all marsupials, the young are born in a relatively undevel-

Table 7.1
A summary of life history attributes for four large possum species.

	Common Brushtail	Mountain Brushtail	Common Ringtail	Greater Glider
Oestrus cycle	26 days	25–27 days	28 days	?
Gestation period	16–18 days	15–17 days	?	?
Annual reproductive rate	0.9–1.4	0.73	1.8–2.4	0.68
Months of most births	Seasonal (March–May +/- Sept–Nov) & continuous	March–May	May to July, +/- Sept to Nov	April & May
Breeding females per year (%)	90	80	90–100	60–75
Age at weaning	6–7 months	8–9 months	6–7 months	7–9 months
Mortality of dependent young (%)	15 (variable)	66	45–95	20
Age of dispersal	8–18 months	18–36 months	8–12 months	10–11 months
Age at birth of first offspring	12–24 months	24–36 months	14 months	24 months

oped state but in the possums they are carried in a well-formed, forward opening pouch after birth. Both brushtail possum species, the Scaly-tailed Possum and the Greater Glider have two nipples and rear one young while the Ringtails have four nipples and mostly raise two young but can raise up to four. Cuscuses also have four nipples and they have been recorded with three young but generally raise only one.

The phalangerids and pseudocheirids belong to the group of marsupial species that have more than one oestrus (egg-producing) cycle each year (polyoestrus) and shed several eggs during ovulation (polyovular) with the gestation period — calculated as the time between copulation and the birth of the young — being less than 60 per cent of the length of the oestrus cycle and coinciding with the luteal phase of the cycle. Some of these larger possum species are monovular but this is thought to be a secondarily derived characteristic.

The structure of the female reproductive tract in possums is typical of marsupials, with paired lateral vaginae and a temporary birth canal which forms for the birth of each young (Figure 7.1). The breeding cycle begins with the enlargement of the ovaries, the growth of the egg follicles and development of the surface of the uterus (pro-oestrus phase). These changes peak at the time of oestrus or 'heat' and mating may occur. The egg is released from the ovary in the first or second day of the oestrus cycle. If that egg is not successfully fertilised, they are able to return to the oestrus cycle and attempt to conceive again. Pregnancy does not affect the oestrus cycle either, but lactation does. If a young possum does not make it into the pouch after birth and does not begin suckling, then the next oestrus will occur at the expected time. If suckling does begin, then the oestrus cycle is interrupted. In placental mammals the oestrus cycle is disrupted by pregnancy.

The time from fertilisation of the egg to the formation of the blastocyst (when the cells start to differentiate) has been shortened so that the formation of the primitive streak (which becomes the spinal cord and brain) occurs by the tenth day. The important organ systems have begun to develop by 13 days and by then the embryo has a well-developed head with a mouth and tongue, front legs with claws, heart, lungs and upper digestive tract. The excretory system and endocrine (hormone) system are slower to develop. The Common Ringtail and Greater Glider appear to have a similar embryonic development to the brushtail. In these species the reproductive tract begins to develop before the external sex organs and the sex of newborn young cannot be distinguished until they are a few days old.

In the uterus, the developing embryo is sustained by the secretion of the hormone progesterone. This is produced by a special gland structure called the corpus luteum, which forms when the egg is released into the uterus. The amount of progesterone produced increases dramatically at the time when the cells of the fertilised egg begin to multiply (the eighth day of oestrus in the brushtail) and drops sharply at the birth of the young (Figure 7.1).

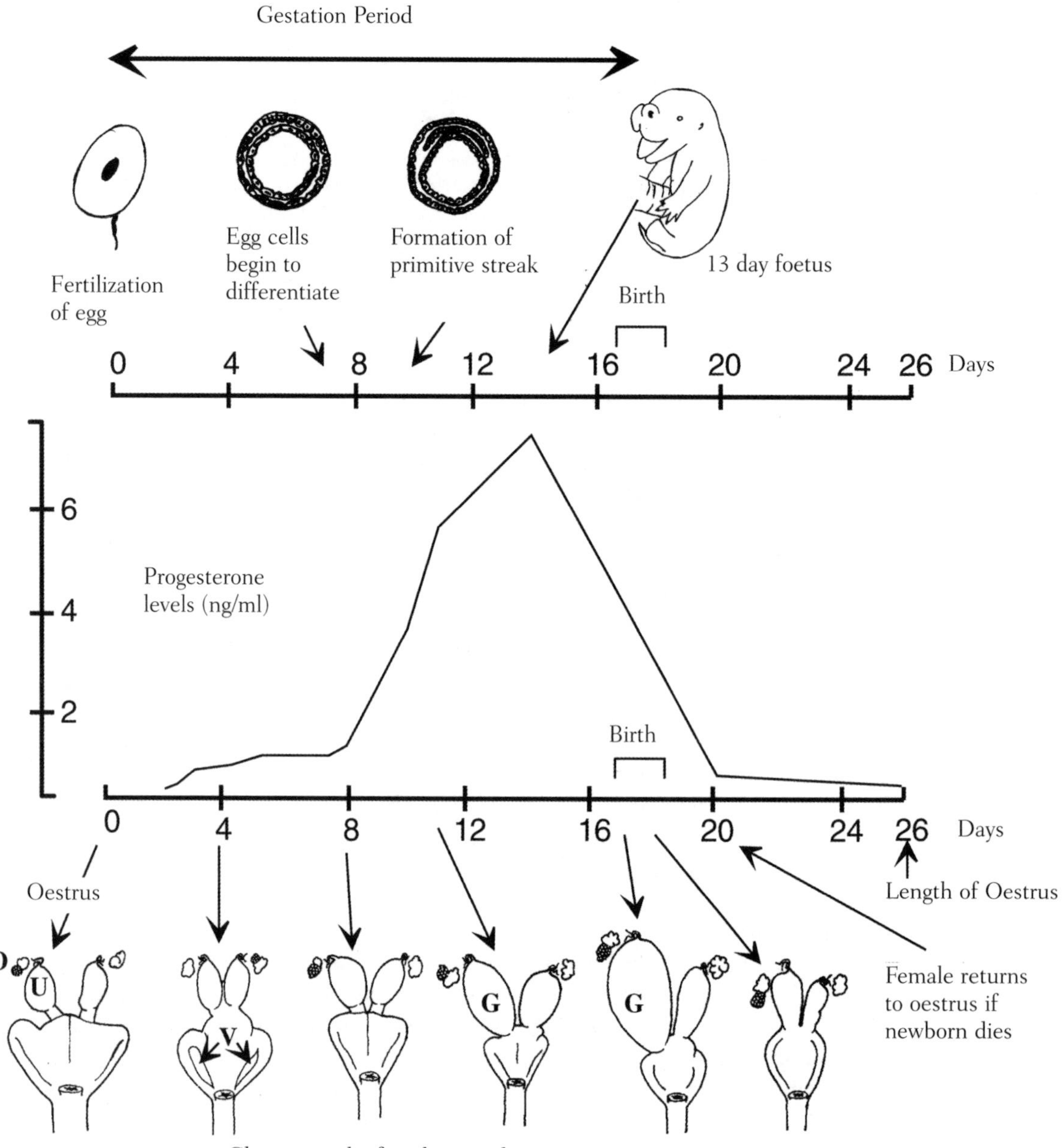

Figure 7.1
Changes in the level of the hormone progesterone in the blood, development of the embryo, stages of the oestrus cycle and morphology of the female reproductive tract of the Common Brushtail Possum (drawn from Hughes and Hall 1984, Pilton and Sharman 1962, Tyndale-Biscoe 1973). O: ovary; U: uterus; G: gravid uterus; V: paired lateral vaginae.

At birth the young leaves the uterus, passes through the medial vagina and then down the temporary birth canal. At this time the female sits on her rump with her tail drawn between the partly extended hind legs. The young is gently expelled by the mother after the loss of some fluid from the urogenital opening. Once outside, the young turns in the direction of the pouch and travels unaided through the fur to the pouch opening and into the pouch. The tiny possum is only a little more than one centimetre in length but the front legs are relatively well developed. This was first observed in 1958 by Gordon Lyne but unfortunately the young possum fell off and did not survive.

The mammary glands are within the female's pouch at about the level of the groin and located just each side of the midline. Each has a single teat and the milk is exuded from some six to ten minute ducts arranged around the apex of the teat. In the Common Brushtail Possum these glands develop and regress in synchrony with the oestrus cycle and both a pregnant and non-pregnant female can feed a newborn baby until it is independent. At birth, both the glands in the Brushtail are fully developed but in the Common Ringtail, which has four teats, the two lower glands are often more developed than the upper two. Possum milk is high in solids, protein, calcium, phosphorus and cholesterol but low in lactose when compared with that of cows and humans. Like other marsupials there are two phases in the milk production. In the first 80 days after birth the young brushtail is permanently attached to the nipple and the sucked gland remains relatively small. After this stage the growth of the young accelerates, the gland can increase to twelve times its size and there is an increase in protein content of the milk, which continues as the young, matures. While there is a suckling young, the female does not ovulate but can return to oestrus nine days after loss or weaning of the young.

Male reproductive system

The structures of the male possum reproductive system are similar to those of other marsupials (Figure 7.2). The vas deferens connect with the paired testes and epididymides, which are in a scrotum in front of the penis. The furriness of the scrotum varies from being naked in the tropical Scaly-tailed Possum to quite dense furring on southern temperate species such as the Common Ringtail and Greater Glider. The temperature of the testis is maintained at about 4°C below body temperature and this is known to prevent the sperm from becoming deformed.

Male brushtails are fertile throughout the year but the size of the prostate gland and the production of testosterone is greater during the breeding season than at other times of the year. In an experimental population in New Zealand, testosterone secretion has been shown to have a marked peak at the onset of breeding, and an increase in the size of the prostate correlated with an increase in serum testosterone. In the tropics, where the northern form of the brushtail breeds continuously, high testosterone levels in the blood appear to coincide with the presence of a female in oestrus and to be higher for the dominant male of the population. The prostate gland is important in the production of prostatic fluid that makes up a large proportion of the ejaculate. This prostatic fluid forms a dense postcopulatory plug in the female after mating, preventing insemination by more than one male. The production of sperm and size of reproductive organs varies seasonally in the Greater Glider and the Common Ringtail.

COMMON BRUSHTAIL POSSUM

Breeding season

Births of Common Brushtail Possums have been recorded for every month of the year but the distribution is highly seasonal except in tropical populations (Figure 7.3). In temperate Australia the main peak of births is usually in autumn but a second peak of variable magnitude occurs in spring. The autumn period is usually from March to May or June. The peak is mostly in April but there is some variation with the peak number of births in Sydney occurring a month earlier than in Tasmania and even a difference of a week or more between adjacent populations has been recorded in NSW and New Zealand.

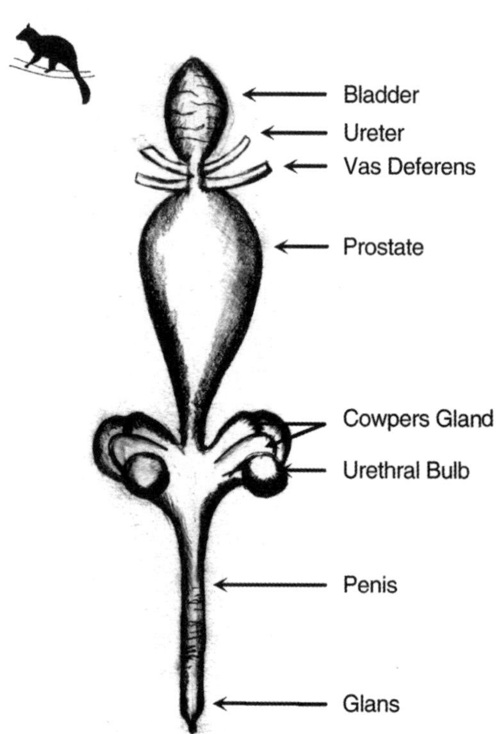

Figure 7.2 Common Brushtail Possum male reproductive system (drawn from Tyndale-Biscoe & Renfree 1987).

The occurrence and size of the spring breeding period shows even more variation. In some locations it was absent or nearly so, while in other areas it was quite pronounced. This spring peak is either the result of breeding by females that failed to breed or lost their young in autumn, or double breeding by successful females. A bigger spring peak corresponds with a higher incidence of double breeding. In the Alligator Rivers Region of the Northern Territory, populations of the Northern Brushtail Possum breed continuously with all females conceiving again before the pouch young is fully weaned.

Control of the timing of breeding in this species is related to a variety of factors. The production of melatonin and a short day length stimulate ovulation, indicating that photoperiod (day length) controls the initiation of breeding. Photoperiod also appears to be important in controlling the fertility of breeding possums and the length of the breeding season, but it does not explain variations between years in one population, between adjacent populations or between regions.

The influence of seasonal food availability has been examined for some populations by comparing the distribution of births with a plant growth

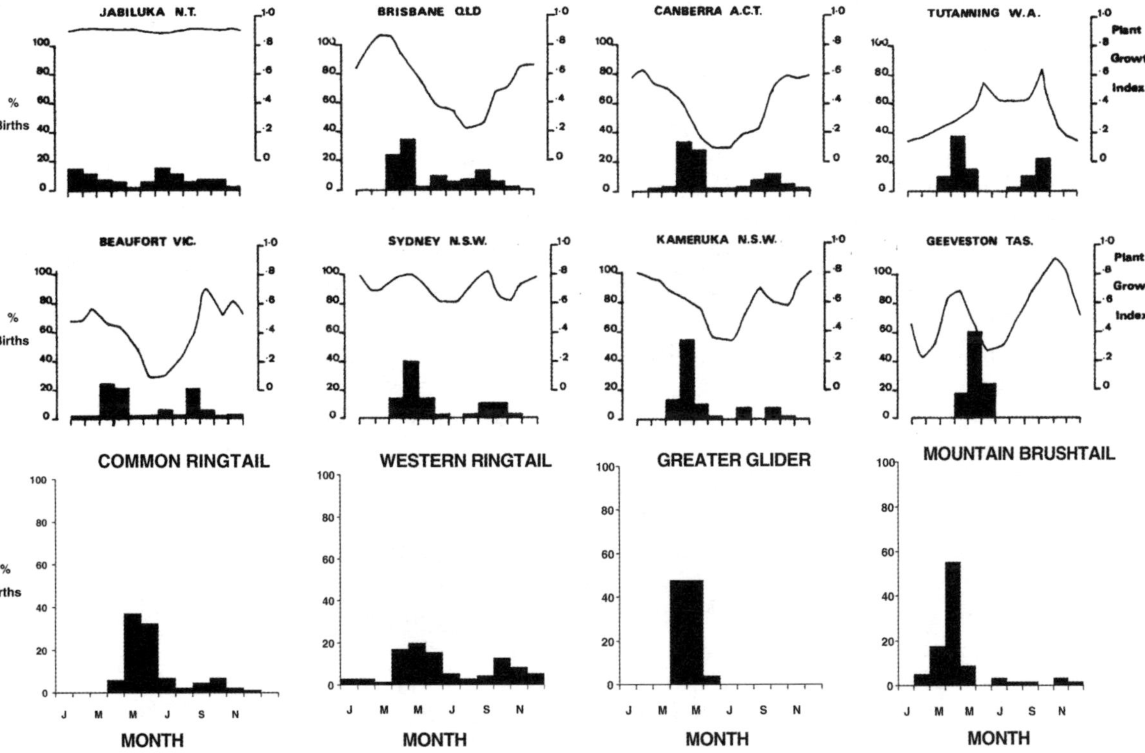

Figure 7.3
Distribution of births of Common Brushtail Possums from eight Australian locations and the plant growth index for the nearest weather station, and of the Mountain Brushtail Possum from Clouds Creek, New South Wales, Common Ringtail Possum from Sandy Point, Victoria and Greater Glider from Tumut, New South Wales (from How 1976, How et al. 1984, Smith 1969).

index based on light, temperature and moisture regimes in the same area. Variation in the plant growth index throughout the year is included in Figure 7.1 and for most populations the spring growth index is highest five to seven months after the autumn birth peak, which is at the time when lactation demands are highest and the young emerge from the pouch. The growth index reflects seasonal variation in foliage production rather than the production of supplementary foods such as flowers and fruits. The variation in breeding season at a local level is probably explained by local site factors including the concentration of nutrients or antifeedants in the preferred foods and the availability of supplementary foods.

The status and condition of the population also seems to influence the distribution of births, especially the size of the spring peak. In the Orongorongo Valley in New Zealand, Bell found a marked variation between years and between classes of females. Females which successfully raised their young bred earlier than unsuccessful females, one- and two-year-old females bred later than older females, and females with a higher body weight bred earlier and more successfully than in years when body weight was lower. In Tasmania, Greg Hocking found that possums recolonising recently burnt habitats bred earlier than those in more stable habitats that had not been burnt for at least eight years.

Oestrus cycle, gestation and lactation

The non-pregnant oestrus cycle of the Common Brushtail Possum is 26 days and oestrus lasts for less than a day. Ovulation occurs within one day of oestrus and unsegmented eggs are present in the oviduct and uterus two days after copulation.

Copulation generally occurs with only one male, and a plug of coagulated semen and vaginal secretions usually fills the vaginal sinus for a day. Gestation period, from copulation to birth, is 16–18 days (17.5 days), about eight days shorter than the oestrus cycle. Ovulation is suppressed by lactation but females can return to oestrus eight or nine days after the loss of a suckling young. Oestrus and conception towards the end of lactation has been recorded occasionally for temperate brushtail possums but always occurs in Northern Brushtail Possums. On rare occasions females have been found with two young in the pouch, 24 days apart in age, indicating that post-partum ovulation can occur. Very occasionally twin pouch young have been recorded. Lactation begins as soon as the newborn young attaches to the teat and non-pregnant females can rear fostered pouch young.

Growth and development

A newborn Common Brushtail Possum weighs 0.2 grams and is 13 mm long (crown–rump length). Although the newborn's weight is less than one ten-thousandth of its mother's, it is relatively larger than a newborn kangaroo, which is a mere one sixty thousandth of its mother's weight. The newborn possum is pinkish and semi-transparent and has a network of blood vessels visible through the skin. The forelimbs are well developed, and all digits on the front paws have sharp claws turned inwards towards the palm. These help the newborn grip the fur when climbing into the pouch. The newborn's tail points between the legs, the ears are fused to the head and difficult to see, the eyes are closed, and it has no fur or whiskers. The nostrils are well developed and the mouth opening is terminal with the lips being fused to form the characteristic sucking mouth of new pouch young (Figure 7.4). The newborn young cannot be sexed because neither the pouch nor the scrotum is visible.

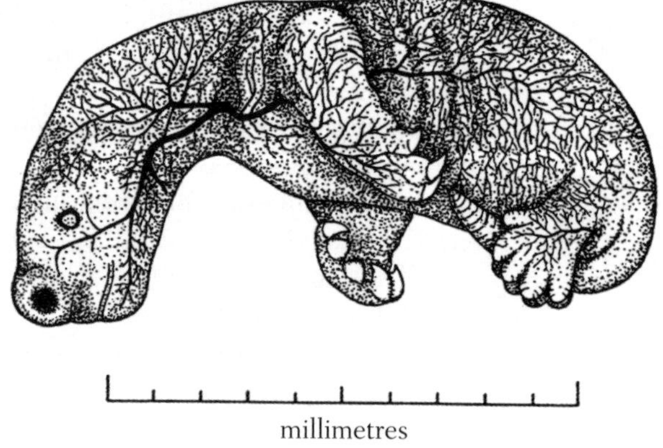

Figure 7.4 Newborn unattached Common Brushtail Possum (from Lyne et al. 1959).

The stages of development of the pouch young are mapped on Figure 7.5 and illustrated by the photos of young aged 41, 96 and 136 days (see plates 13–16). By 40 days the tail is free and prehensile, the ears have formed but the eyes are still closed. The young will begin to release the nipple when about 80 days old and the eyes will open from 100 days. This is the period when there is a change in the quantity and composition of the milk produced to accommodate the demands of the rapidly growing young. When they are about 120 days they are well furred and may begin to leave the pouch while the mother is in the den. After 140–150 days they no longer return to the pouch but will ride on the mother's back while she feeds (Plate 18).

Weaning can occur from about 140 days but mostly occurs when they are between five and seven months and weigh 350–600 grams (Plate 17). At that time the young loses weight. The pouch of the weaned female is shallow with nipples inverted and covered by a black scale. The nipples are everted at 260–300 days (750–100 grams) and full pouch development occurs at 270–350 days (940–1110 grams). In males, testes usually grow to adult size quite suddenly at about 12–14 months of age and sperm are produced. Females can breed when 12–14 months old but this varies between populations. In one Western Australian population they did not breed until they were three years old. The young leave the maternal den from seven to 16 months, with males leaving earlier than females.

Figure 7.5 Developmental stages of the Common Brushtail Possum pouch young.

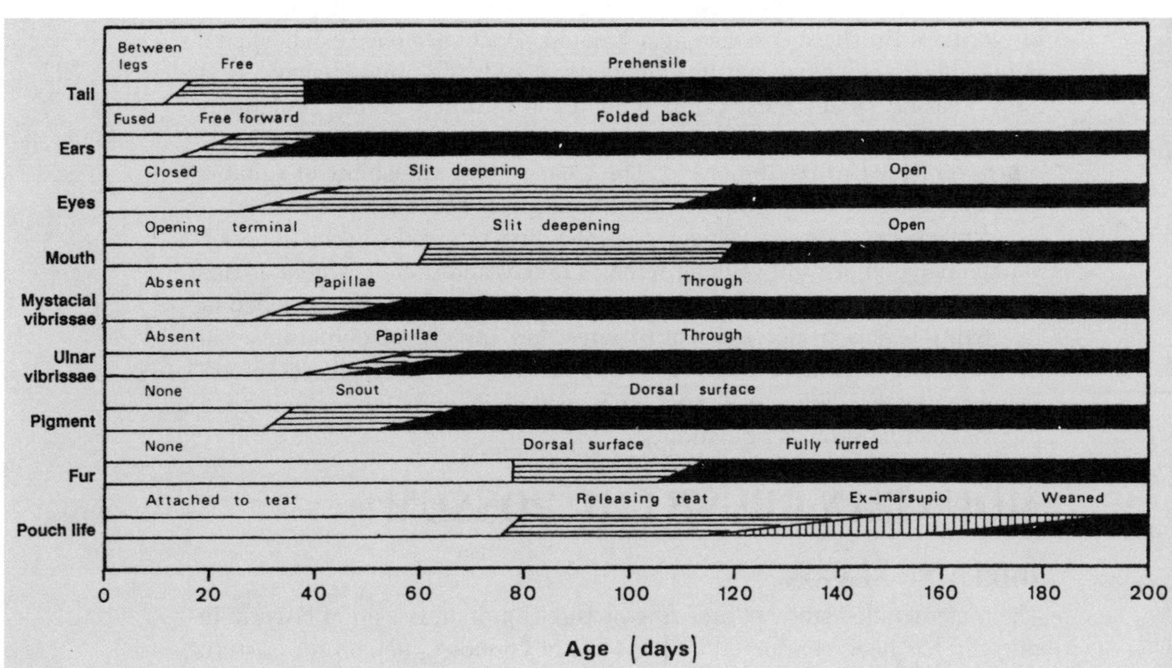

Population dynamics and regulation

Social structure varies between Common Brushtail Possum populations. Mortality of pouch young is generally low with survival rates of 87 per cent in Australia and 85 per cent in New Zealand. Less than 18 per cent are lost in the journey from birth into the pouch. There are usually the same numbers of male and female pouch young (sex ratio around 1:1). Differential mortality of the young after weaning results in the sex ratio of adults varying from 3:1 (males to females) to 0.4:1.0. The proportion of immatures within the population is also variable, ranging from 10 per cent to 32 per cent. The recorded lifespan of Common Brushtails is two to 14 years, most of these being captive individuals. The oldest record of 14 years has been determined by counting tooth cementum layers and a mean life expectancy of 6.7 years has been calculated for wild populations in New Zealand.

Some of this variation in population structure seems to be related to habitat quality. In Tasmania, males were found to be more abundant in populations colonising recently burnt forest but there were equal numbers of males and females in populations from more stable habitats. A higher proportion of males was also evident in populations recovering after poisoning operations in New Zealand and in an increasing Northern Brushtail Possum population. Young males are capable of dispersing over long distances — the longest recorded being 12.8 kilometres — and one- to two-year-old males are most common in colonising populations in New Zealand. In established populations males are recruited from outside the population while young females may not leave their birth population at all. Neither males nor females remained in their area of birth in the population of Northern Brushtail Possums near Kakadu. Once they have established a home area, they have some site fidelity. In a study of homing behaviour in New Zealand some translocated individuals returned home, sometimes more than once. At one site, four animals travelled 3.9 kilometres while others remained where they were. The location and availability of suitable nest sites were the most important influence over homing behaviour.

While population size is increasing, the birth rate and survival of pouch young is high, more and younger females breed, and there is a greater survival of immatures. Once the carrying capacity of the habitat is reached or its quality begins to decrease, birth rates and survival of immatures will decrease. Resource-dependent factors appear to be of much greater importance in the regulation of Common Brushtail Possum populations than external factors such as predation.

MOUNTAIN BRUSHTAIL POSSUM

Breeding season

The most detailed study of breeding by the Mountain Brushtail Possum in the wild has been conducted by Ric How at Clouds Creek on the eastern escarpment of the New England Tableland in north-eastern New South

Wales. Births were recorded in all months except January, June and October but 87 per cent of births occurred in the four months between February and May, and the peak of this season was the 10 April (Figure 7.3). Only one young was raised each year. Occasional births outside this time were second pregnancies after the death of the first young and only one followed the successful weaning of the first young. Not all females bred every year.

Oestrus cycle and gestation

The reproductive cycles of this species and the Common Brushtail Possum are very similar. It is polyoestrus and monovular and the oestrus cycle is 25–27 days (mean: 26.4). The gestation period (oestrus to birth) is 15–17 days (mean: 16.2) and twins have been recorded, but very rarely. They returned to oestrus ten or 11 days after the loss of a pouch young.

Growth and development

The developmental stages of the pouch young are similar to, or occur later than, the Common Brushtail. Growth of the whiskers on the snout (37 +days), the fur (95–110 days) and opening of the eyes (112–120 days) all occur later. The young emerge from the pouch when 155–210 days, mostly between 175 and 200 days after birth and begin riding on their mother's back. They remain dependent for the next two to three months and are not weaned until they are at least 240 days old. The Scaly-tailed Possum also has a longer pouch life than the Common Brushtail.

The nipples evert when the females first ovulate at the end of the second year. Prior to that the nipples are covered with a black scale and the pouch is just a depression. They are sexually mature at the end of the second year but only half will reproduce then and these early breeders seldom rear their young beyond pouch stage. The remainder do not breed until they are three years old.

Population dynamics and regulation

In How's study at Clouds Creek, Mountain Brushtail Possums formed monogamous pairs and inhabited an overlapping home range for most or all of the year. There, the ratio of males to females from birth through to adult was 1:1 indicating that there was no bias in the survival of the young. Survival of offspring was low with 52 per cent of pouch young surviving to an age of about six months and 44 per cent to weaning. Dispersal of young occurred from 18–36 months and females left earlier than males. The presence of a dependent immature possum appeared to adversely affect the development of a pouch young which sometimes died before weaning, decreasing the survival rate. However, a more recent study of the Mountain Brushtail Possum in Victoria has found that the adult sex ratio was female-biased (1.4 females per male) and this ratio differed between the sexes in each age group of possums.

They are relatively long-lived with females averaging nine years and individuals up to 17 years old having been recorded. Males have an average longevity of 6 years with the oldest being 12 years. At Cambarville, two individuals were trapped within 250 metres of their original trapping site after eight and nine years. The reproductive rate, longevity and social structure suggest that it is a species with a self-regulated population occupying stable habitats.

COMMON AND WESTERN RINGTAIL POSSUMS

BREEDING SEASON

Births in Victoria occur in all months from April to December but most are between May and July with a smaller spring peak (Figure 7.1). There is an initial consort period before mating when the male follows, grooms, forages with, and later nests with, the female. The first litters of the season are born to established pairs in which the female has previously reproduced and the pair may mate again in late October and produce a second litter in mid to late November. Females that have not bred before give birth a month later. This timing is not consistent throughout the range of the species. In north Queensland most females give birth at the beginning of the season while around Sydney there is a high incidence of spring breeding.

In south-west Western Australia births of the Western Ringtail Possum occur in all months but most are in winter (April to July). A second peak of births occurs in September to November (Figure 7.1). At one population the first peak represented 60 per cent of births with 20 per cent in the spring peak while another population had a more even distribution with 44 per cent in autumn and 38 per cent in spring.

OESTRUS CYCLE, GESTATION AND LACTATION

The Common Ringtail has the most typical reproductive pattern of this group of marsupials — it is polyoestrus and polyovular. The oestrus cycle is about 28 days long but the length of the gestation period is unknown. Up to six eggs may be shed during ovulation and there is a record of five young in the uterus but usually only one to three eggs are fertilised. The Common Ringtail Possum can have from one to four young in a litter with two being the most frequent and four very uncommon. The Western Ringtail mostly has one young with twins representing about 10 per cent (ranging from none to 17 per cent) of births.

The second peak of births is a result of breeding again by females that have lost their young and females that have successfully reared their first litter. It is mostly from 'double breeding' because the loss of an entire litter is rare. Females that successfully rear two litters have the first litter earlier in the season, wean the young earlier and have a greater body weight. Those breeding for the first time do not have a second litter that season and the number of females breeding twice varies between years. Milk changes in composition throughout the pouch life of the young with total solids remaining low throughout but being highest at 15 weeks, as is the concentration of milk proteins and sugars.

Males are not reproductively active all year with the testes regressing and producing less sperm outside the breeding season.

Growth and development

The newborn Common Ringtail is a little larger than the Common Brushtail being 0.3 grams in weight — a ratio of about 1:3000 between a single newborn and the mother — and with a crown–rump length of 15 millimetres. It has a strongly developed head and shoulder region, especially the forelimbs and is generally similar to the newborn Common Brushtail.

The pouch life lasts for about four months. The young can begin releasing the nipple when they are 42 days old and begin to vocalise when they are 60 days. The eyes open after about 100 days and at that time there is a sparse covering of fur over the body and they can clearly vocalise. At 105 to 112 days they are sometimes found out of the pouch but leave permanently after 120 days when they weigh 65 to 90 grams. Lactation mostly stops when the young are 180 to 220 days old (about 26 weeks) but it can happen as early as 140 days and as late as 34 weeks. The presumed father has also been observed to assist in caring for the young in the last couple of weeks before weaning by grooming, staying with the young while the mother forages and warning of potential predators.

Females become reproductively mature and reach adult weight in the winter of the year following their birth. Most begin breeding when they are 14 months old although some breed when they are 13 months. The males mature a little earlier, in the autumn following their birth.

Western Ringtail Possums begin to emerge from the pouch at about 95 days when they weigh 125 grams and leave permanently at about 104 days and 130–150 grams. They continue to suckle for six or seven months (550–650 grams). Adult body weight is reached at about eight to nine months and females are reproductively mature at about ten or 11 months with first births being recorded for two females when they were 305 and 320 days old. Compared with the Common Ringtail Possum, the Western Ringtail has a faster growth rate, its young leave the pouch sooner and at a larger size, and it can reproduce when younger.

Population dynamics and regulation

The seasonal distribution of Common Ringtail Possum births enables late lactation and weaning to occur at a time when the abundance and quality of food and the weather favour growth and survival of both mother and offspring. In addition, the breeding potential (fecundity) of this species is the highest of all the large possum species. The Common Ringtail Possum is quite gregarious with family groups often sharing nests and some care of the young. This may be important in increasing the survival of young possums.

Mortality rates of juveniles are generally low during pouch life but can increase significantly soon after independence. At Lysterfield in southern Victoria, Lester Pahl found that 26–80 per cent survived to weaning and 30 per cent to sexual maturity during years of average rainfall but as few as 6 per cent survived to weaning and 2 per cent to sexual maturity during drought years. Other studies record the survival of 74 per cent of males and 84 per cent of females to weaning, with most being lost once they began to leave the pouch, and 25–55 per cent survival to sexual maturity. Mortality decreases in the second and third year followed by a sharp increase in individuals lost in the spring and summer of their fourth year. Some adults are known to have lived for six years but most do not survive for more than three.

Although sex ratios are equal at birth, ringtail populations mostly have more females than males but this varies between populations and age groups. Female survival was always higher than in males at Lysterfield, while at Sandy Point male and female survival were similar in the first year but thereafter more females survived. There were equal numbers of adult males and females in the Warramate population.

The annual reproductive rate varies between individuals, years and populations and within populations. In populations with high adult survival there are high proportions of females that have bred previously and more litters can be produced in spring although the proportion of 'double breeding' varies between years. The reproductive strategy appears to be one that is partly seasonal and predictable and partly opportunistic — the April to August breeding is predictable, the double breeding is opportunistic.

Dispersal and recolonisation by Common Ringtail Possums has not been studied in detail. Adults and their offspring have rarely been found outside their established home ranges and some removal experiments indicate that recolonisation of 'vacated areas' does not occur rapidly despite animals of dispersal age being present in the adjacent population.

The reproductive strategy of the Western Ringtail Possum has some notable differences from the Common Ringtail. There is no nest sharing except between females with young and there are fewer young produced but these can grow more quickly and mature earlier. Longevity is unknown but some females have been known to breed for three successive years. Barbara Jones found variation between populations that reflects differences in habitat quality. In one population (Locke) 70 per cent of all age classes were female, twins were more common, the young grew faster, more young were born in spring and density was double that of the other population (Abba). At Locke, dreys were the usual nest site, but at Abba they preferred tree hollows and competed with the sympatric Common Brushtail Possums. Overall, the Western Ringtail has a lower reproductive potential and this may be reflected in a poorer ability to survive adverse conditions.

GREATER GLIDER

Breeding season

The breeding season of the Greater Glider, from March to June, is the most restricted of these species, with almost all births occurring in April and May. Any young that are lost are not replaced so there is no second peak of breeding. Only 60–75 per cent of adult females breed each year.

Oestrus cycle and gestation

The length of the oestrus cycle and gestation period of the Greater Glider are unknown. Because of the restricted breeding season they have only a single oestrus (monoestrus) although they are physically capable of being polyoestrus. The males produce sperm only during this brief breeding period and the testes regress after May, so if a female fails to breed at the first oestrus or loses a young they do not conceive again. They have only one young.

Growth and development of pouch young

The young remains in the pouch for four to six months and then is left in the den or sometimes carried on the mother's back for another three or four months until it is weaned in January or February. They are independent at eight to ten months but do not become sexually mature until their second year.

Population dynamics and regulation

The reproductive potential of the Greater Glider is lower than for the other species. With the first breeding not occurring until the second year and only 60–75 per cent of adult females producing a single young, the reproductive rate is only 0.67 per female per year. The mortality of dependent young is relatively low at only 20 per cent and is male biased, changing the sex ratio from 1:1 at birth to two males per three females at the time of weaning. The reproductive success is greater amongst females living in forests with higher levels of nutrients. The life span of this species is unknown but is estimated to be at least four years in order to maintain the population size with the reproductive rate being less than one.

Breeding partners share den trees from February to October but males may be either monogamous or bigamous, depending on the quality of the habitat. In southern Victoria, Steve Henry found that polygynous males had significantly larger home ranges than monogamous males. Males maintained exclusive access to associated females but occasionally pursued other females. They do not share dens during the period when the young are being left in the nest. The process of juvenile dispersal is not known but adult males are thought to be agonistic to male offspring and may drive them away at an early age causing deaths amongst young males.

Greater Gliders have a lower fecundity and lower juvenile mortality than Common Brushtail and Common Ringtail Possums and this results in a stable population, well spaced through the forest. Like the Common Ringtail Possum, they are slow to recolonise 'empty' habitat.

CHAPTER 8

INTERACTIONS BETWEEN POSSUMS

The most common image of these large possums is of an individual sitting in a tree staring down, its bright eyeshine gleaming. Alternatively the Common Brushtail and Ringtail Possums are known from their nocturnal activities as they move noisily around a garden or house. They are mostly alone but occasionally are accompanied by their young. The arrival of a second possum, especially a male, usually leads to the first one leaving or some hissing or spitting. You might also be aware of their musty odour, especially if they have been living in the roof cavity.

DAILY ACTIVITY

Almost all of the large brushtail and ringtail possums and cuscuses are strictly nocturnal, rarely emerging from their dens or nests during daylight hours. The only exception is the Green Ringtail Possum, which does not use a den or nest and although mostly nocturnal has been observed to feed and move about during the day. The Daintree River Ringtail is also known to sleep without a nest as well as in tree hollows and may be active during daylight hours.

Common Brushtail Possum

Activity begins in the dens one or two hours before sunset, with possums emerging about half an hour after sunset if the weather is suitable. Heavy rain may delay emergence by up to five hours. For the next couple of hours they remain in the den tree grooming, sitting or moving about. Between 10–22 per cent of the nightly activity is occupied with feeding and an individual usually feeds at two to four sites in one night. The distribution of the time spent feeding varies, from continued feeding throughout the night, to two or three main sessions separated by periods of inactivity. Overall 45 per cent of time is spent sitting, 10–20 per cent grooming and 20–30 per cent on other activities such as travelling between feeding sites. The number of active possums is usually highest between 11 pm and 2:30 am. They return to their dens just before dawn in summer but several hours earlier in winter. Females tend to return to dens a little earlier than males.

The proportion of time individuals spend in five main activities throughout the night has been determined by Doug MacLennan after many hours observing fifty possums near Brisbane (Figure 8.1). Their solitary behaviour was reinforced by the very small amount of time involved in active social interaction, which was greater during the breeding season. Conversely, the proportion of time spent sitting, doing nothing, is quite high. Time spent feeding peaked six hours after sunset.

They spend up to 15 per cent of their active time on the ground, most of which they use travelling, in addition to feeding and sitting. Grooming and any social interactions take place in the trees. They are more active on the ground during moonlit nights although the moon does not affect their overall activity levels. Windy conditions reduce activity levels, as does heavy and persistent rain. Coppery Brushtail Possums on the Atherton

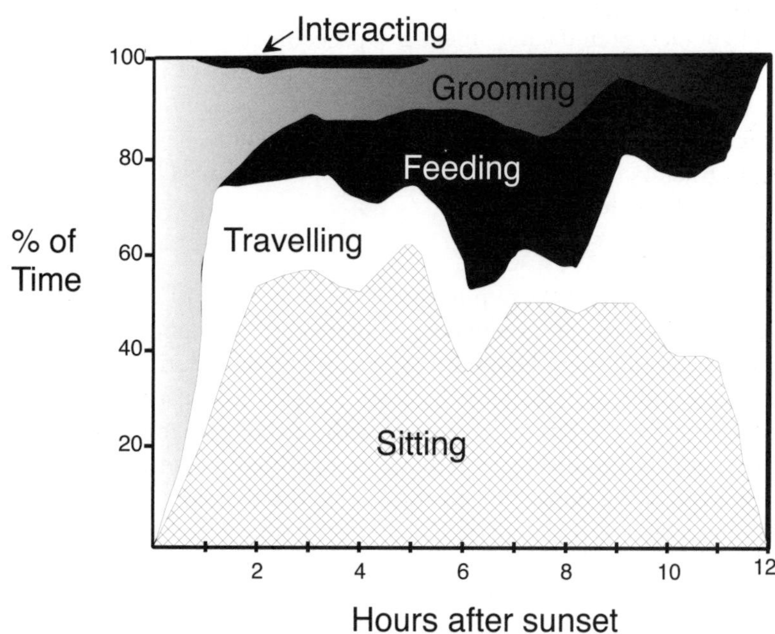

Figure 8.1
This diagram shows how a Common Brushtail Possum occupies its time when outside its den (after MacLennan 1984).

Tableland significantly reduce their activity on cooler nights (below 14–16^{0}C). Predators also affect activity with a finding that a reduction of fox numbers resulted in possums significantly increasing the time spent feeding and moving on the ground.

Common Ringtail Possum

Common Ringtails leave their nests during twilight and are most active until midnight, before the air temperature drops to its minimum for the night. In the central highlands of Victoria they emerge from tree hollow nests forty-five minutes or so after dusk. Their activity is reduced more by wind than light drizzling rain, while heavy rain or cold fog may completely suppress normal activity. They will only leave their nests during the day in very hot weather. Near Melbourne, Lester Pahl observed them leaving their dreys and sitting in shaded parts of the canopy when the maximum temperature reached 37^{0}C. On the Atherton Tableland, the activity of the Herbert River and Lemuroid Ringtail Possums was reduced on clear and moonlit nights and with cooler temperatures.

COMMUNICATION

Communication signals send information about physiological and behavioural condition between individuals. Signals are transmitted in a variety of ways: smells, sounds, visual clues and aggressive interactions. They can be used on their own or in combination. Touch is also used but little is known about this. It has been mostly described in association with courtship, mating, contact between the mother and the young and grooming of each other. The Rock Ringtail Possum especially seems to engage in a lot of physical contact. Sounds and smells are probably most important in long-distance communication and establishing the spacings of individuals, and touch and visual cues are more important for close-contacts. The most detailed studies of communication in large possums have been of the Common Brushtail Possum carried out on captive animals by John Biggins and in the wild by John Winter.

Sound

The Common Brushtail Possum is one of the most vocal of marsupials, and most possum species can produce a complex set of calls and sounds. Deep guttural coughs and sharp hisses are especially common during the breeding season. Most of the described vocalisations are used as threats during aggressive contact or are used to make contact with surrounding individuals.

The unique structure of its larynx is undoubtedly associated with the brushtail's very vocal behaviour. In the larynx, the thyroid cartilage is dilated, forming a rigid walled spherical chamber about the size of a pea, which has a 1.5 mm circular opening through the floor of the larynx. It is thought that this acts as a resonating chamber and both brushtail species have notably loud calls.

The Common Brushtail Possum has a rich variety of some 18 sounds. They grunt-growl-hiss-screech when threatening another brushtail, use a buccal click when startled or stressed and have a unique chattering call and clicking sounds for close contacts including mating. The calls of the Mountain Brushtail are similar to the Common Brushtail but the male mating calls differ quite markedly, a fact well known to professional trappers. The only recorded call of the Scaly-tailed Possum is a chittering and chirruping when startled. This is more like a ringtail than the calls of the more closely related brushtails. Cuscuses generally use harsh screeches and clicks. Other calls such as hissing, coughing, snorting, squeaking and hooting have been described for the Ground Cuscus in New Guinea with the squeaks having an unusual hint of harmonics.

The ringtail possums and Greater Glider have a smaller repertoire of sounds, are less vocal and have relatively soft calls, compared with the brushtails. Ringtails are most vocal in aggressive encounters or when an infant becomes separated from the parent. When active, they produce a high-pitched chirruping twitter, which is used to maintain contact with other individuals. The Greater Glider has a variety of calls: guttural grunts, shrieks or gurgling shrieks used during threatening interactions or when startled, and a juvenile separated from its mother uses a slow hissing. Female Common Spotted Cuscuses announce the onset of oestrus with a loud braying.

Threatening vocalisations in possums appear to be complex with considerable variation in their intensity and duration and the same sounds seem to be emitted by both dominant and defeated individuals. Common Brushtail Possums have a series of graded sounds and John Winter has suggested that this indicates the existence of a high degree of social organisation.

Smell

Possums have a variety of scent glands that can provide information about the identity, sex, reproductive condition and social status of an individual. They are thought to help with synchronising breeding behaviours, maintaining bonds between the young, the mother and family groups, and defining territories. The most detailed studies have been of the Common Brushtail Possum with 11 scent-producing glands identified. These are found in the mouth and the pouch, on the ear, chin and sternum, around the cloaca and between the digits.

Scents are deposited by rubbing the chin and sternum, wiping the mouth and dragging the cloaca on branches or other objects and by dribbling urine as the possum moves around. Identifier odours are used to mark and define ownership of a territory; emotive odours produced by a white sticky secretion are released in response to fear; and reproductive odours are from vaginal mucus smeared on branches by oestrus females.

Advertising territory boundaries is often described as an important reason for scent-marking by possums but they do not maintain exclusive territories. Odours are probably more important in helping a resident animal learn its home range. The more familiar a resident is with its surroundings, the more self-confident and successful it will be in any aggressive encounters; an intruder is more easily intimidated in unfamiliar areas. Scent-marking probably also influences the relative spacing of individuals.

The sternal gland is found on both males and females of the brushtail species and the secretions produce the familiar dark orange/brown coloured stain on the chest. Production of the sternal secretion in males is controlled by the level of testosterone in the blood and its use differs between males and females. It also becomes more oily in the breeding season. Sternal rubbing can happen at any time and they prefer to mark objects less than half a metre above the ground. Male Common and Mountain Brushtail Possums have a similar scent from the anal gland and each one reacts to the scent of the other species.

All five of these large possum species and the Common Spotted Cuscus have paracloacal glands at the base of the tail that produce an often foul smelling sticky white secretion especially when the possum is frightened. These potent glands are a hazard for anyone trapping possums for research! They are larger in sexually active males and there are two pairs of glands, except in the Greater Glider, which has only one pair.

Paracloacal secretions are distributed by cloacal dragging and large quantities are secreted when an animal has been defeated and assumes a submissive posture. The two types of glands differ in their relative sizes between the Mountain and Common Brushtail Possums, suggesting differences in social behaviour between these two species. In Common Brushtail Possums the oil-secreting glands are only a little larger than the cell-secreting glands while Mountain Brushtails have substantially larger oil secreting glands. Male Rock Ringtail Possums have very large paracloacal glands (two centimetres in diameter) and have special marking sites. These are frequently visited patches of rock with a dark glossy coating smelling strongly of urine and faeces (Plate 18).

Saliva is another source of scent signals for Common Brushtail Possums, which spend a lot of time washing and grooming. When washing the face these possums spread saliva over the inner surfaces of the forearms, which are then dragged forwards from the ears along the side of the face towards the nose. It also involves the use of the syndactylus claws, which are combed through the fur, then repeatedly licked clean and occasionally forced into the corner of the mouth adjacent to the glands. Grooming with saliva may have a secondary function of covering the animal with its own smells and spreading information about identity, family relationships or physiological state.

SIGHT

Possums communicate visually using acrobatics, tail waggling or sweeping, display of pale body colours, and body position. The displays most commonly used are the threat and submission postures during aggressive interactions. The position of the ears appears to reflect the emotions of an individual — ears at an angle of 100 degrees: alert; vertical: anxious or perplexed; horizontal with the white tips visible from the front: anger, pain, fear or pleasure. In most instances, visual signals do not operate alone but are used to strengthen the impact of the vocal and scent cues. Visual communication is not restricted to displays made by the animals during close contact: marks left by chewing, gnawing and scratching are more permanent signals of activity than the deposition of odours.

AGGRESSIVE ENCOUNTERS

In the Common Brushtail, aggressive interactions are generally initiated when one animal, usually the more dominant, approaches its opponent who responds by adopting a threat posture. This begins with a quadrupedal stance in which the body is lowered, the head extended forward, and the ears lowered horizontally and directed forwards. Exposure of the light coloured underside might be an important visual signal between these nocturnal animals. Movement from a quadrupedal to a tripedal and then a bipedal stance represents a graded series of threat postures increasing in intensity and is accompanied by a series of sounds. Threat calls are performed with an open mouth, exposing the prominent lower incisors — another important visual signal.

If a defeated individual is unable to escape quickly, it will assume a submissive posture in which it lies on one side with all four legs stretched out and release large quantities of the white secretions from the paracloacal glands. This posture appeases the victor and stops further attack.

In most cases interactions between Common Brushtail Possums involve 'give way' procedures, which include calls and an upright body stance with no body contact. Occasional fights that include body contact and chases occur and these are most intense between males. The outcomes of previous encounters markedly influence the behaviour of animals during interactions between familiar opponents. Encounters between unfamiliar individuals are influenced by their initial levels of aggression and readiness to interact socially as well as their relative familiarity with the environment in which

Figure 8.2 Some aggressive postures of the Common Brushtail Possum (from John Winter).

(a) Low intensity raised paw threat

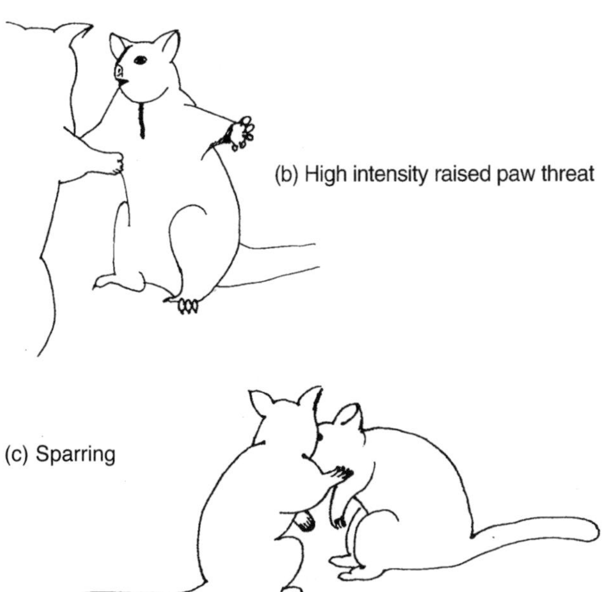

(b) High intensity raised paw threat

(c) Sparring

the encounters occur (Figure 8.2). In captive studies the majority of aggressive encounters were between the dominant and subordinate males.

John Winter has suggested that Common Brushtails have a social system based on threatening encounters in which the maintenance of a minimum distance between individuals is highly developed. Dominance hierarchies are established between males in captivity and fights have been observed between females around dens. The arms are held apart during aggressive interactions. In most cases encounters between individuals are mild with direct contact being avoided while they peer silently at each other with ears erect.

The Greater Glider, Common Brushtail, Mountain Brushtail and Common Spotted Cuscus all use bipedal threat postures to inform their opponents of the likelihood of being attacked. These postures are used also by subordinate Common Brushtail Possums, and the submissive posture has some elements of the defensive threat: an open gape, hiss-screech vocalisations and extended forelimbs and forepaws. Aggressive reactions of the Common Spotted Cuscus include harsh screeching and lashing out with forelimbs held low in front of the body. Males of this species cannot be housed together in captivity.

There is apparently less aggression between Common Brushtail Possums from arid and tropical regions. In central Australia, Aboriginal informants say that sometimes males will fight over a female but not over food or territory. The Northern Brushtail Possum is also much less aggressive than its eastern counterpart, readily sharing dens in the wild and nest boxes in captivity.

During the courtship period for Common Brushtail Possums it is necessary for the male to overcome the female's preference for being alone. They have a consort period of about 30 days when males approach and withdraw using the soft calls of juveniles. This then allows mating to occur without fighting.

SOCIAL ORGANISATION

The social organisation of possum populations reflects the size and quality of the habitat: the distribution of food and resources, and changes in the habitat over time. Population size and structure, group size, distribution through the habitat and even the mating systems can all vary with habitat quality. Population density can influence group size, home range and nest sharing. Home area can vary from being a defended territory when resources are limited or, if hollow trees are uncommon, a defended nest tree, to a core home area surrounded by a home range that varies in size and shape in response to seasonally available food supplies. Polygynous breeding is more common in habitats with concentrated or clumped food resources and monogamy more likely with sparse and evenly distributed resources.

Group size and social behaviour

In the forests of eastern Australia, Common Brushtail Possums are generally solitary, both when feeding and in dens, although a consorting male may share a den with a female in oestrus. In New Zealand an individual possum typically uses 11–15 dens in a year and changes dens frequently although there are a few favourites. Dens are often used sequentially by several possums unless there are few suitable den sites available in the habitat. There are also records of dens occasionally being shared by up to five individuals. An exception to this is co-operation and sharing between females and their young. Males defend their access to a group of females but may tolerate one subordinate male in his first breeding season. Females only mate once in the season but males have sequential consort relationships.

In the more unpredictable environments of the arid woodlands and tropical open forests the family groups seem to stay together. In central Australia, Aboriginal informants told Lynn Baker (p 31) that:

> Wayuta [Common Brushtail Possums] live in families with the male staying with the female and young possums. Each family has its own place for sleeping. Sometimes a single adult male might be found in a hollow tree, or just a female with little ones. The young possums move out and set themselves up in a new place once they grow up. A family group may have an extra adult female, other than the mother, but never another male, even if it is a son.
>
> When there were lots of Wayuta Anangu [Aboriginal People] would catch maybe four or five every night.... often after cutting out the hole the boys might find not just one but three or more possums in the tree.

Similarly Big Bill Neijie told me that in the Kakadu area they often find five or six Northern Brushtail Possums within one hollow tree.

The size and type of home area occupied by Common Brushtail Possums varies throughout their broad distribution. The area varies from 0.7 to 42.7 hectares (see Chapter 5) and has variously been described as a defended territory, a home range and a core home range. In most populations studied, home ranges overlap suggesting that there is no defence of territory. This is particularly evident for the Northern Brushtail population near Kakadu in which the population density was three per hectare and males and females all had overlapping home ranges (Figure 8.3). Near Canberra males maintained almost exclusive territories as they did in a population near Brisbane. There, the population densities were just over two per hectare and high-ranking males and females occupied exclusive home ranges (Figure 8.4). Unlike the relatively homogeneous tropical habitat, the Canberra possums lived in remnant open forest with a very patchy distribution of trees. In New Zealand bimodal or 'dumbbell' shaped home ranges occur in which the possums den in one area and move some distance to another area to feed.

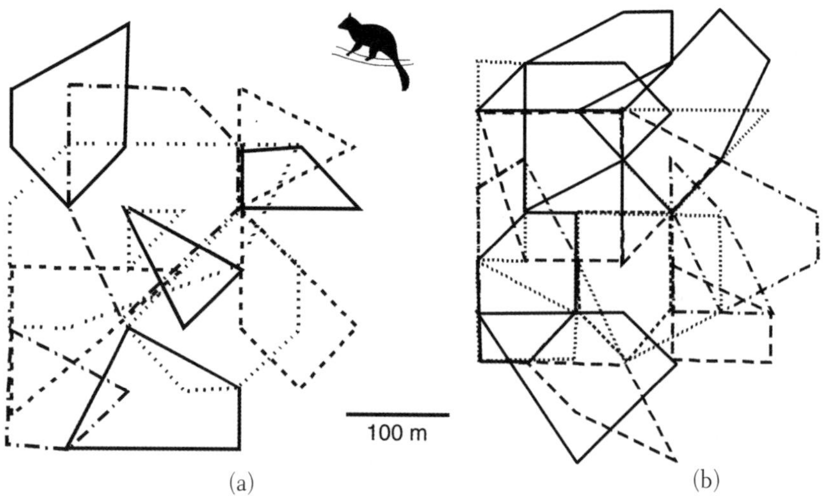

Figure 8.3 The small overlapping home ranges of Northern Brushtail Possums from a trapping study near Kakadu National Park (a) females; (b) males.

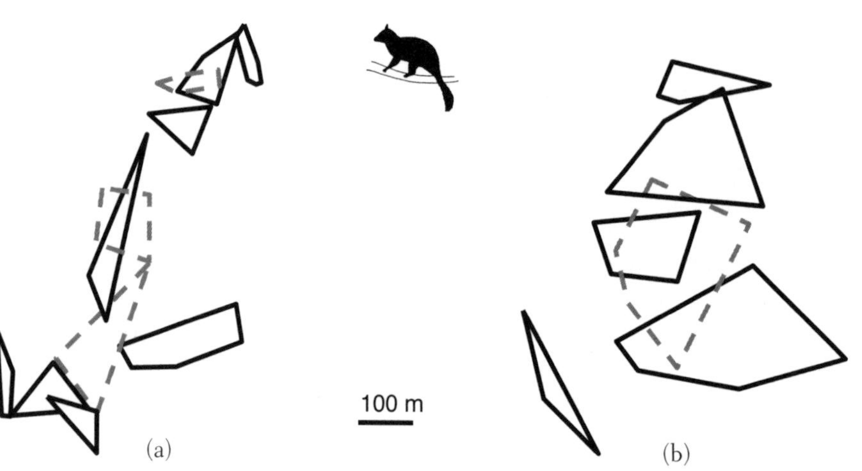

Figure 8.4 The larger more separated home ranges of Common Brushtail Possums in patchy woodland near Canberra (a) females; (b) males (from Dunnet 1964).

Two studies of Mountain Brushtail Possums have found differing forms of social organisation. In northern New South Wales they have monogamous pairs that share a common central home range. They may also feed together, as suggested by occasional captures of an adult male and female in the same trap. In central Victoria they may not be monogamous, with considerable overlap in the core ranges of many pairs. Sharing of dens is also quite common with up to nine other possums. Mostly an adult pair will be found together but sharing by two individuals of the same sex, especially males, is not uncommon and there have been groups of three or four adults together on the same night. Many of the records of three or four animals in one den were during very cold weather and this behaviour may help maintain body temperature. Juveniles remain with their mother for up to three years.

Within the ringtail possum species the group size varies from a solitary existence to small groups. The Lemuroid Ringtail is the most gregarious rainforest possum with groups of two or three individuals being common and records of up to six together being observed. The family groups — an adult male, adult female and young — are cohesive, resting together and drawing together when disturbed. Both the Herbert River Ringtail and the Green Ringtail are solitary but the Green Ringtail has a longer association between mother and young whereas juvenile Herbert River Ringtails have a short period of dependency. The Rock Ringtail Possums move in strongly cohesive groups of two to ten individuals with the young travelling between the adults.

In the southern part of its range the Common Ringtail Possum is gregarious and social interaction is centred on the dreys. At some times of the year groups can contain an adult male, one or two adult females, and their dependent young, as well as the immature offspring from the previous year. Up to five possums of different ages and both sexes may share a nest. Each 'nest group' of animals may use two to four different nests, all of which are located within a relatively small area and kept in good repair. But nests are not always shared and at Sandy Point individuals nest on their own about 50 per cent of the time throughout the year, while in October, 30 per cent of dreys are occupied by pairs, and in October, November and December 30 per cent have three or more individuals. In the Sydney area, the pair bond between male and female remains throughout the raising of the litter and the male will carry the young on his back when flushed from the nest during the day, but in northern Queensland where tree hollows are the preferred nest site and dreys are uncommon, the group sizes are smaller and the possums are less gregarious.

In captivity, male Western Ringtail Possums caged together will fight whereas peaceful combinations were composed of a female and her offspring, including mature daughters. Adult males are mostly not tolerated by mature females. This behaviour may reflect a social organisation that differs from that of the Common Ringtail.

The Greater Glider is a solitary species for most of the year. During the mating season males live close to their females or share their den and maintain exclusive access to particular females by a combination of female defence and resource defence. The breeding system has been defined as 'facultative polygyny'. In high quality habitat that can support more than two animals, males are bigamous but they were monogamous in small patches of forest or poor quality forest. The home ranges of males do not overlap but there is overlap between males and females, and the home range of bigamous males overlaps with both the female mates (Figure 8.5).

Infant–parent behaviour

For most possums it is the female that cares for the young. There is a relatively passive relationship between the female and the young of the Common Brushtail Possum, with interactions mostly limited to the young being washed by the mother, or by being allowed to catch up when following, and the mother responding to juvenile distress calls. Parental behaviour may be more developed in the Mountain Brushtail Possum because the young are dependent for much longer. Male Greater Gliders have no involvement in raising the young.

Parental care is important in the Common Ringtail and care of the young by adult males has been documented by Perry Ong in Victoria. Adults pair at the onset of breeding in late April, groom each other, share nests, and forage together for two to three months. Males then move in with other females without partners. When the young first leave the pouch they are left alone in the nest while the mother forages; later they emerge and ride on her back. For the last weeks of dependency the young travel on the back of the presumed father, nest with him and are groomed by him while the mother forages elsewhere. When the first litter is weaned the pair may mate again and the male divides his time between the mother and juveniles, sometimes accompanying the sub-adults when they disperse and helping them to construct a drey. They will nest with sub-adults until next breeding season when they return to mate.

Parental care is also implicated for some of the other ringtail species, especially the more gregarious species such as the Rock Ringtail Possum and the Lemuroid Ringtail, as well as those with a long period of dependency such as the Green Ringtail. Myfanwy Runcie has observed some fascinating behaviours with Rock Ringtail Possums. Once the young become sure-footed on the rocks, they will bound between the parents and embrace them. This is especially common between the male and young. In general there is a lot of physical contact including grooming within the family group.

Figure 8.5 Greater Glider home ranges in Gippsland Victoria (a) Females, which frequently overlap, and (b) males, which do not overlap with other males (from Henry 1984).

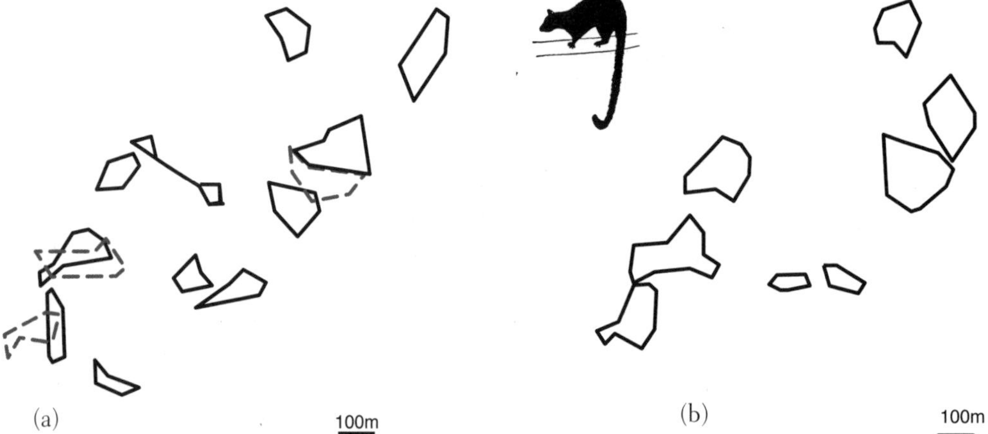

CHAPTER 9

LIVING WITH POSSUMS

ARE POSSUMS COMMON?

The environmental and economic disaster created by the introduction of Common Brushtail Possums into New Zealand is well known and often highlighted, even in Australia. They are undoubtedly a pest in New Zealand and need to be controlled, but are they common in Australia? They can be pests in some urban situations, and they have substantially increased in numbers in Tasmania and on Kangaroo Island, but in the remainder of Australia they seem to be gradually disappearing. In central Australia and Western Australia where they were once common they are now rare. Even in areas where Common Brushtail Possums might be expected to be common, such as the south-eastern forests of NSW, they are less abundant than the threatened Yellow-bellied Glider. Of 930 records of seven arboreal species in 5606 hectares of the south-east forests 40 per cent were Greater Gliders, 4 per cent Yellow-bellied Gliders, 3 per cent Common Brushtail Possums and 3 per cent of Common Ringtail Possums.

The distribution and abundance of all the large arboreal folivores has decreased significantly in Australia in the last 200 years and is continuing to do so. These species evolved in an environment with large areas of continuous forests and woodlands. There was mostly a gradual change in forest type across the landscape but there were some 'habitat edges' such as between rainforest and open eucalypt forest. They survived with periodic fire, some extreme climatic conditions (droughts) and native predators. Now they live in a landscape that has been extensively cleared, with only small island patches of suitable habitat remaining; in habitats altered by grazing; with a fire regime that has changed in frequency and intensity, and with an increasing abundance of feral predators and competitors.

In general, the smaller the geographical range and number of preferred habitats (habitat span) of a species the more likely it is to become extinct. The ability of a species to survive human impact is also related to a variety of other factors such as its population density, ability to disperse across unfavourable habitat, to adapt to change in its habitat and to recover from unfavourable conditions. At present only one species, the Western Ringtail Possum, is described as rare. If it were still classified as part of the Common Ringtail species, it would be considered common! Of the 12 other species, those living in eucalypt forest or woodlands are all described as common or abundant, the two restricted to rocky habitats in the tropics are common with limited distribution and the rainforest species vary from being vulnerable (Lemuroid Ringtail) to sparse with a limited distribution.

The great contraction in range and overall abundance of the Common Brushtail Possum since European settlement is surprising. It has a highly flexible life history strategy that can respond to the suitability and carrying capacity of the habitat. By varying its life history and behaviour it can persist in a wide range of natural habitats, recolonise disturbed areas and colonise novel environments. And yet it is no longer common through much of its natural habitat. In Victoria, the Common Brushtail Possum is considered to be secure but it is not as common as it once was in the north and west of the State. In the Pilliga Forest in central western New South Wales it has changed from being an abundant species to very uncommon in the last four years. Even a great survivor like this seems to be overwhelmed by the continuing contraction of preferred habitat and the impact of feral predators.

The Common Ringtail Possum is described as widespread within its distribution and generally thought likely to remain common despite having lost a substantial amount of habitat. Its distribution has always been restricted to eastern Australia and Tasmania and the availability of suitable nest sites is considered to be a significant factor in limiting its distribution and abundance. Overall change in its abundance has not been assessed but there is evidence that it its distribution is contracting. It has gone from the Eyre Peninsula in South Australia where, according to Aboriginal people, it was once common, and in Queensland it is disappearing from open forest and woodland on Cape York Peninsula. Again, in the Pilliga Forest where they rely on tree hollows for nests, its abundance has also changed from common to rare in four years. During this period forestry activities have continued, targeting the important hollow-bearing trees like the Narrow-leafed Ironbark. Although the Common Ringtail has the highest reproductive rate of these large possums it does not readily recolonise vacated habitat, which restricts its ability to recover from habitat disturbance, the impact of predation and unfavourable weather conditions.

Both the Mountain Brushtail Possum and the Greater Glider are more restricted in their preferred habitats and distribution than are the two 'common' species and in some areas have been able to maintain high densities. But neither of these species has an especially flexible life history strategy nor do they readily recolonise vacated habitat. Changes in the distribution and abundance of Mountain Brushtail Possums have not been generally assessed but it is inevitable that they have declined as a result of habitat destruction and past harvesting for skins. The habitat occupied by a population of Mountain Brushtail Possums studied by Ric How in the 1970s at Clouds Creek has now been replaced by a pine plantation and David Lindenmayer was unable to compare it with his Victorian population. Greater Glider populations do not survive clearfelling of large coupes for timber, and their preferred forests are those with high-quality timber resources and fertile soils favoured for pine plantations.

These four species, which occupy eucalypt forests and woodlands, are not in imminent danger of becoming extinct. They are all found in National Parks. But many local populations are threatened or extinct and it is important that the broad picture of their decreasing distribution and abundance continue to be monitored so that they do not decrease to unacceptable levels without it being noticed.

POSSUMS IN YOUR GARDEN

> 'The common Opossum...has learned that the space under the roof of the usual type of suburban bungalow affords an excellent shelter, and in such situations it freely takes up its residence. In this enterprise Opossums have earned the ill will of the suburban householder, as their activities are nocturnal and noisy.' Frederic Wood Jones (1924)

Abundance of urban possums

Both the Common Brushtail Possum and the Common Ringtail Possum co-exist with humans in the urban environment but the Brushtail is the most notorious. In Melbourne John Seebeck found both to be common, with Ringtails mostly restricted to the eastern side of Melbourne, which has more gullies and suitable vegetation than the western part of the city. Both species were happy to nest in buildings. There have been no other studies of urban Common Ringtail Possum populations.

A survey of the eastern suburbs of Adelaide revealed that 35 per cent of households reported having Common Brushtail Possums and 25 per cent of households with brushtails reported property damage. Most of the damage was caused by eating fruit and ornamental plants (61 per cent), 20 per cent was structural and 7 per cent electrical. The leafy well-established suburbs of Adelaide are prime brushtail real estate with plenty of nutritious foods, secure dens and protection from fires and predators. Deaths on the road are their greatest problem.

In Launceston a detailed study of urban Brushtails was conducted in two areas — one of about two square kilometres around the CBD and another suburban location with a corridor to a large reserve. The 28 possums trapped could cover quite large areas, from 0.3 to 42.1 hectares and used 80 different places to rest in during the day. Roof cavities were used for dens more often than other sites (24 per cent) such as chimneys, under buildings, in buildings and occasionally in trees. Eleven of the study possums were killed or injured on the roads.

Living with urban possums

Both the Launceston and Adelaide studies concluded that it would be impossible to permanently remove brushtail possums from the suburban garden and that it is better to learn to live with these native rogues despite their sometimes anti-social behaviour. Wildlife education programmes are essential in the management of urban possum populations.

Trapping of 'pest' possums and their removal to a patch of natural bushland some distance away has long been common practice. It has long been assumed that if taken far enough away they would settle into their new surroundings and be 'better off' than if they remained in the garden; but if not taken far enough they would return to their original 'home'. In Launceston this assumption was found to be invalid: relocated individuals did not return but either disappeared or were killed on the road. In Melbourne, Rod Peitsch tracked relocated brushtails only to find that most died within the first week after they were released, killed by foxes, cars or by the stress of being moved. The remainder were lost, probably being pushed out by the resident possums of the release area. So, rather than being the kind treatment it is often assumed to be, relocation is quite inhumane.

An easier and more humane solution is to prevent brushtail possums from entering roof cavities and to provide alternative nest sites in the surrounding area. All new houses and housing additions can be built to 'possum proof' specifications. For an existing building:

- find the point of entry (which can be quite small) by watching the animals or by using lights in the roof cavity;
- block it securely as brushtails are strong and can be very persistent — ensure that the possum is not locked inside, do a temporary repair while they are out at night, and secure the hole properly during the day;
- sprinkle camphor or naphthalene flakes, spray with quassia tea, or wash with bleach around the hole and roof area to disguise the possum scents;
- put a light in the roof cavity for three days and nights;
- remove branches from trees that provide easy access to the roof;
- if access is via power lines you can attach an 80-centimetre diameter disc over the wire close to the facia board of the building;
- ensure all roof tiles are sealed — possums can lift loose tiles;
- provide an alternative den site by putting up nest boxes (Figure 9.1) as there are rarely any tree hollows available in the urban environment.

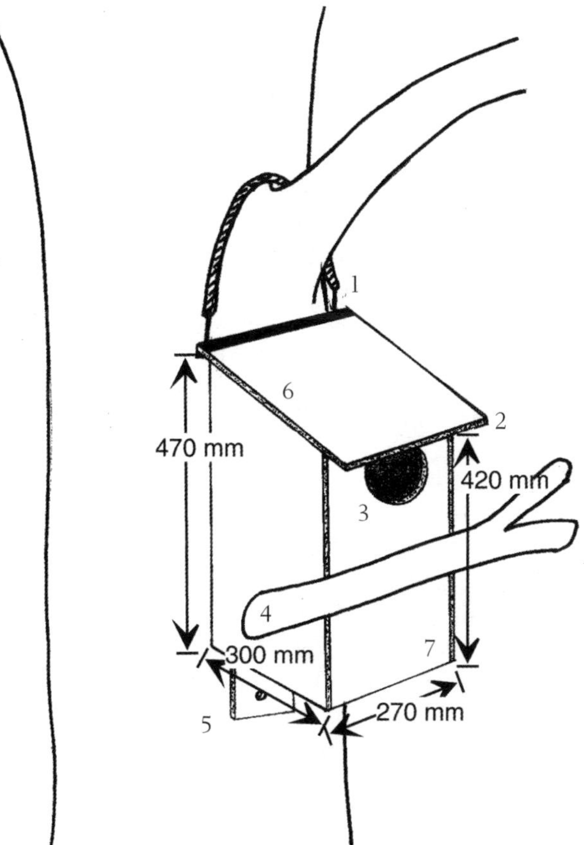

1 Make the top edge of the lid weatherproof – use old inner tube as a rubber flap;

2 Hinged lid needs to overhang front of box by 100 mm;

3 Entry hole needs to be just under the lid and doesn't need to be circular; width of hole needs to be about 120 mm;

4 Attach a strong branch to the front of the box for the possum to hold on to;

5 Secure the box firmly to a tree, attaching it at the top and the bottom;

6 Do not use chipboard for the box because it will disintegrate too quickly;

7 Drill drainage holes (<10 mm diameter) near each corner of the floor of the box;

8 Make sure all other gaps are blocked to keep the box as dark as possible;

9 Some nesting material (dead leaves, woodshavings) would provide extra insulation.

Figure 9.1 Design of a nest box suitable for brushtail and ringtail possums in your garden.

In the garden you can reduce their destructive feeding binges on your favourite roses by spraying the plants with a cold solution of quassia tea made from quassia chips stocked by some chemists and health food shops. It is a bitter tea that makes the plant undesirable, but be warned — I have known an angry possum to attack and shred a plant that had been sprayed with quassia! You could also provide an alternative food supply by hanging some apple and bread in a nearby tree and hopefully protect a special plant. Another approach is to cover plants with wire netting or to provide aerial runways with rope or timber, which directs the possum away from plants you want to protect. It is also important to train your dog not to bark at possums. Teach the dog to live with the wildlife and not disturb the neighbours.

If removal of possums becomes unavoidable you must remember that they are protected species and cannot be removed without a permit from the State or Territory wildlife authorities. In most cities there are pest control companies licensed to trap and relocate possums using approved humane methods. It is illegal to harm them in any way. It is usually cheaper and preferable to learn to live with our native wildlife than to remove them to an almost certain death. In addition, the removal of a pest possum may not solve your problem because another will probably move in and occupy the vacated territory.

You may occasionally find a stray dependent young that has become separated from its mother, or an adult injured by dogs, cats, cars or electrocution. There may also be a young still alive in the pouch of a dead female. If you do find an injured possum cover it with a towel or put it into a pillowcase and gently place it in a dark place such as a box. Do not handle the animal or show it off to your friends. It will be frightened and may cause you or itself an injury. If it is a pouch young, wrap it in a soft cloth and keep it close to your body to keep it warm or it will lose body heat very quickly.

Rather than trying to care for or rear these possums yourself it is preferable to contact someone from an organisation such as the Wildlife Information and Rescue Service (WIRES) in New South Wales, the RSPCA, or other approved organisations. Members of these organisations are trained in the care and handling of native animals and the regulations that cover their care and release. You could also take it to a vet who may be able to help an injured possum or advise you of an appropriate contact. Rescuing some injured or misplaced animals can be difficult and you may require help. If you do wish to provide the care then you must be aware of the special needs of the animal and the wildlife laws for your State or Territory and be prepared to give a lot of time to the task. Check the phone book for wildlife care organisations near you. Barbara Smith also provides a list in her book *Caring for Possums*.

POSSUMS IN THE WILD

THREATS TO SURVIVAL

The complete loss of habitat resulting from large scale land clearing in Australia, fragmentation of habitat, and the loss of nest sites, coupled with adverse weather conditions, frequent hot fires or an influx of predators, severely affects the survival of possum populations. When assessing the potential impact of forestry activities, clearing or other land management procedures these factors must be considered in combination.

Logging and clearing continue to be the greatest threats to possum populations in eastern Australia. In the coastal forests near Bega, Dan Lunney found that logging significantly reduced the numbers of Greater Gliders, which were then further reduced by burning of logged coupes especially during drought. Gullies, including all drainage lines, are extremely important for the survival of species and must remain unlogged. In an area of wet sclerophyll forest near Tumut (NSW) Greater Gliders did not survive a clearfelling operation. Most of them died within one week and the few survivors were those whose home range had not been completely destroyed. They made no apparent effort to move to suitable adjacent habitat. A dramatic reduction in the numbers of Common Brushtail and Ringtail Possums has also been found following forestry activities in the Box–Ironbark forests near Chiltern in north central Victoria and the Pilliga Forest in New South Wales. In addition to the loss of important trees, these activities destroy the understorey growth that is so important to some of these species.

In central Australia, where the Common Brushtail Possum has almost disappeared, large scale clearing cannot be blamed for the population collapse. An explanation of this decline is only possible when a range of factors is considered in combination (Figure 9.2). Before European settlement possums occupied small areas of quality habitats scattered throughout this environment. During periods of favourable conditions, possums dispersed into sub-optimal habitats, but when struck by drought these populations were the first to be lost and only those in prime habitats survived. This cycle was broken with the arrival of European settlement. Many of the preferred possum habitats were destroyed by stock and rabbits; more animals were killed by predators and by extra hunting for skins; and populations were reduced to a level that could not survive both the natural and added impacts. It is difficult to find a reason for the major collapse of Common Brushtail Possum populations in central New South Wales and Queensland late last century (see Chapter 2) but a combination of factors like this would seem to be the most likely scenario.

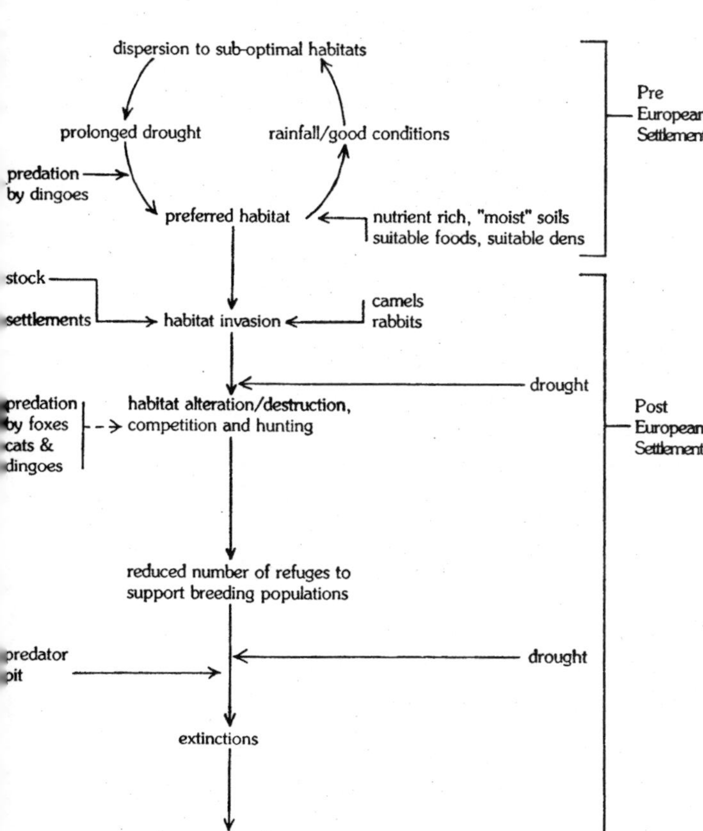

Figure 9.2
Possible sequence of events that resulted in the decline of the Common Brushtail Possum in the arid zone. The cycle at the top represents the system operating before European settlement. The combined impact of drought and disturbance follows from this.

The Common Spotted Cuscus, Herbert River Ringtail and Lemuroid Ringtail Possums are vulnerable to the impact of logging and disturbance in their isolated habitat patches. The Rock Ringtail and Scaly-tailed Possums can fall easy victim to a predator invasion and late dry season firing of bush around rocks. Burning, local grazing and clearing will all affect the short and long term food supply of rock dwelling possums.

PREDATION AND COMPETITION

The impact of predators varies throughout the year and with population size. Juveniles and dispersing young are more vulnerable than adults and small populations are more susceptible than larger populations. Predation by dingoes, cats and foxes has often been considered an important cause of species decline but in many cases both dingoes and cats co-existed with the possum species long before the serious decline occurred. In some areas, especially the arid and semi-arid parts of Australia, predators can have a serious impact at particular times such as at the onset of a drought and when population size has been severely reduced. At such times, even a low level of predation can keep a population in a so-called 'predator pit', preventing the population from returning to a sustainable size. Predation is therefore likely to be instrumental in the final demise of a population that has already declined rather than being the cause of the original decline. Foxes, dingoes, dogs and cats are now the most significant predators of large possums although they are still preyed upon by native species such as large owls, goannas, pythons, quolls and Tasmanian Devils.

Foxes, dogs, dingoes and cats prey on all arboreal animals. The importance of possum in their diet varies greatly but the consumption of Common Ringtail and Common Brushtail can be very high. These are the species that are frequently on or close to the ground. In Croajingalong National Park in Victoria, where ringtail possums are very common, they represented 58 per cent of fox, 56 per cent of cat and 38 per cent of dog diets. Brushtail Possum represented only three per cent of the dog and fox diets in this study and was not eaten by cats but in other studies they were 35 per cent of the diet of dogs. Where rabbits are common the proportion of possum eaten is much lower. The fox is probably the prime cause of the extinction of the Western Ringtail Possum in inland areas of its former distribution. They are known to pull these possums from their dreys and to have killed about 15 per cent of a population within three months.

Where predators are present, Common Brushtail Possums alter their behaviour and minimise the risk of predation. At Lake Burrendong, Common Brushtail Possums spent less time on the ground, travelled shorter distances, reduced time spent active and avoided open areas if foxes were present or if fox scents were placed on the ground in habitat without foxes. Brushtails were able to discriminate between old and new fox scent. Where the possums have to come to the ground in discontinuous habitat they are more exposed to predators.

The only predator known to consistently eat Brushtail Possums is the Dingo. They are most likely to catch dispersing young and those that have not successfully established a home range. The young rejected from the maternal nest use less secure dens such as hollows near ground level if the better dens are all occupied — population density and habitat quality indirectly determine the number of individuals susceptible to predation.

Powerful Owls are a persistent enemy of Greater Gliders and Common Ringtails and depend on them for food. The owl swallows the possum head first, followed by the entire animal including the skin and skeleton back to the base of the tail. They reject the tail and skin flaps from the thighs containing the anal glands. In the Healesville area north-east of Melbourne David Fleay reckoned that a pair carried off one Greater Glider or Ringtail almost every night and John Seebeck has estimated that a pair of Powerful Owls might consume 250 Common Ringtail Possums in a year. They have also reduced a Greater Glider population from 80 living in 100 hectares of forest to eight individuals during a period of 46 months. From this, Rod Kavanagh suggests that Powerful Owls concentrate their hunting in pockets and then move to another area when their prey becomes too scarce. They will also eat brushtail possums, mostly in spring when the young are becoming independent and an increase in their predation of ringtails in summer probably also reflects the ease of catching young animals. Rufous Owls prey on the rainforest ringtails.

Other known predators of the Common Ringtail Possum are the Lace Monitor, goshawks and Wedge-tailed Eagles. Brushtail possums are also preyed upon by large pythons, large goannas and Tasmanian Devils. For some possum populations, especially those in urban areas, there is an additional 'predator' — motor vehicles — with many possums being killed on the road.

There is competition between possums and a variety of other animals. In central Australia rabbits have a direct impact on the Common Brushtail Possum with a substantial overlap in their diets, especially when there is fresh plant growth after rain. Destruction of the understorey by stock also removes some of plants that are important at particular times of the year. Even feral bees may pose a significant threat in areas with a shortage of mature hollows. In a two-hectare site in the You Yang Ranges west of Melbourne, feral bees occupied 25 per cent of all hollow bearing trees and 8 per cent of hollows. Characteristics of the hollows used by both bees and Brushtail Possums overlapped and very few of the remaining vacant hollows were suitable for possums, although more were available for bees.

PARASITES

A variety of mites, ticks, fleas and internal parasites have been found in both free-living and captive possum populations, although only the Common Brushtail, Mountain Brushtail, Southern Common Cuscus and

Herbert River Ringtail Possum have been studied in any detail. In general there are few parasites in wild populations, especially internal parasites. They do pick up some additional parasite species when feeding in and around agricultural lands, such as a nematode worm usually associated with rabbits. Toxoplasmosis (a protozoal disease that attacks the nervous system) also seems to have been acquired by accidental ingestion of spores where there have been infected cat faeces, as it is not recorded from possum populations outside human settlement.

Nineteen species of mites, ten tick and ten flea species have been found on Common Brushtail Possums — but no lice. Mite infestations can cause various skin irritations, scabs around the eyes, nose, ears and tail as well as a 'mange'. Ticks have been found only on Australian brushtail possums, not on possums in New Zealand. They generally cause skin irritation, anaemia, or toxaemia and may carry other diseases. They may cause paralysis of their hosts although the Common Brushtail appears to have a resistance to their poison. Fleas can also cause local inflammation, anaemia and allergic dermatitis, and they act as vectors of disease. Rumpwear, or more accurately *lumbo-sacral dermatitis*, is commonly found on possums in Tasmania and New Zealand. This condition is manifested as baldness or matting of the fur, thickening of the skin and sometimes scab formation on the rump. It appears to be an allergic reaction associated with flea or mite infestations. Internal parasites have been found in captive Common Brushtail Possums, cuscuses and Scaly-tailed Possums but the number found in free-ranging possums is very small. Most are uncommon and some apparently do not affect the animal.

MANAGEMENT OF POSSUMS

Conservation management

The Western Ringtail Possum, a listed rare species, is the only one of these large possum species that has specific conservation protocols. Rehabilitated possums have been released into the Leschenault Peninsula Conservation Park north of Bunbury since 1991. This program has established a self-sustaining population in a secure conservation estate.

Conservation of arboreal possums in the forests and woodlands of eastern Australia requires an understanding of the appropriate patch size, length, width and composition of corridors, the density and characteristics of hollow-bearing trees and feeding requirements. Present management prescriptions for clearing and logging include recommendations for the minimum patch size and the number of hollow-bearing trees to be retained but there have been no long-term studies of whether these prescriptions enhance the survival of possums and other forest inhabitants. There is also no long-term information about the impact of regular control burning on possum diversity and abundance.

The minimum size of remnant patches and maximum area of clearfelled coupes required for the continued survival of all possum species will vary across the range of their habitats. A high level of both floristic and structural diversity is essential: Greater Gliders require the maintenance of a high eucalypt leaf biomass in the upper canopy; the Mountain Brushtail lives where there is a high diversity of plant species and a dense understorey; Common Brushtail Possums prefer the drier habitats; and Common Ringtail Possums are most abundant where there is a dense understorey of wattles and other shrubs. Patch size must also allow for seasonal variation in habitat use. Preferred food plants have a regular cycle of new leaf growth and flowering and this results in a pattern of movements of the possums around their habitat as they search for food. The complex forest mosaic and tree species diversity must be maintained.

The life history strategy and population dynamics of a species also determine the size of remnant patches it needs. David Lindenmayer has analysed the stability of Mountain Brushtail Possum populations and found that a single population is more likely to survive than a number of small populations even if their total size is equal to the original population. Greater Gliders are relatively common in undisturbed forest but their abundance is reduced and they have a patchy distribution through regenerating forest and pine plantations. They do not seem to survive logging unless part of their home range is retained, and large forest remnants and corridors are required, including gullies, for their conservation in logged forest.

The retention of wildlife corridors in wood production forests will assist some species but be of little value for others. In the Victorian montane forests Greater Gliders were present in surveyed corridors as frequently as they were in continuous forest whereas the Mountain Brushtail Possum populations did not occur as commonly in corridors as expected. The value of the corridor will be determined by the suitability of the habitat it contains. If there are not enough suitable tree hollows or a sufficiently wide range of food sources the possums will not survive. The corridors need to cover the range of topographic variation in the area, from the ridge top to the gully. They also require management because forest resources are not static through time, being affected by factors such as drought, fire frequency and natural succession. Regular control burning, for example, will have a significant impact on the density of the understorey and wetter forest associations, reducing the habitat suitability for Common Ringtail and Mountain Brushtail Possums.

Hollows in eucalypt trees develop only in older trees, mostly when they have a diameter at breast height of more than 100 centimetres and may be 50–200 years old. In Blackbutt trees, hollows suitable for large possums only develop when the trees are about 200 years old. If the timber-harvesting programme in an area has an 80–120 year clearfelling rotation then it is unlikely there will be enough time for sufficient new hollows to develop, resulting in the loss of the hollow-dwelling possums and other fauna. The type and number of tree hollows needed by each of the four large possums vary (Table 9.1).

Table 9.1

Tree hollow requirements of Common Brushtail Possums, Mountain Brushtail Possums, Common Ringtail Possums and Greater Gliders in south-eastern Australia. Some of this information is based only on one study (after Gibbons and Lindenmayer 1997).

	Common Brushtail Possum	**Mountain Brushtail Possum**	**Common Ringtail Possum**	**Greater Glider**
Number of hollows/hectare	0.4–11.0	More than 3–5	2–15	1–26
Height of hollow entrance	> 6 metres	24 metres	4 metres	8–40 metres
Entrance diameter	more than 10 cm	12–25 cm	6.5–8.0 cm	8–18 cm
Hollow depth	9–12 cm	28 cm	more than 20 cm	28 cm
Diameter at breast height	55–143 cm	?	20–143 cm	54–200 cm
Uses dead trees?	?	Yes	?	Yes

Management prescriptions usually require that 3–16 hollow bearing trees per hectare be retained but there is little direction about the species, size, form or health of the preferred trees. In some cases the retained trees are kept in clumps (a convenient arrangement for the loggers), in others a tree may be left surrounded by a small patch of vegetation. Information about the Mountain Brushtail Possum population in the montane forests of Victoria suggests that a clumped distribution of trees may not be suitable as they prefer trees with a large number of hollows not surrounded by dense vegetation. This will vary between habitats and possum species.

In addition to protecting existing hollow-bearing trees it is essential to retain younger trees to replace the older trees. At present the type, species and location of trees to be retained is determined largely by guesswork and requires more analysis across the range of habitats. A variety of characteristics describing the crown, stem and age of a tree need to be taken into account. The retained trees then need to be protected. In some parts of the landscape they appear to be more likely to collapse after logging has been completed or they may be destroyed by burning off. While irregular fires help hollow formation by facilitating decay, intense or repeated fires such as control burning, destroy the hollow-bearing trees.

Installation of nest boxes in forest with a shortage of hollow trees has been suggested as a useful management tool successfully used in Europe. This should be considered only as a last resort because it is expensive in installation and maintenance costs and although possums will use nest boxes their suitability for the ultimate survival of the population has not been assessed. It will always be preferable to retain suitable trees but in some logged forests nest boxes may already be needed for the survival of species. The smaller Leadbeaters Possum is an example of this.

The presence of possums can have an added advantage in woodland and forest management by controlling the growth of potentially destructive parasitic mistletoes. They generally have more succulent and nutritious leaves than the host trees and are a favoured food of both the Common Brushtail and Common Ringtail Possums. Brushtail possums preferred mistletoe to a selection of eucalypt leaves and other foods in experiments conducted by Queensland Forestry in the 1930s and mistletoe is a preferred food in other diet studies.

Control of mistletoe has both an environmental and economic benefit particularly in areas with highly disturbed, fragmented forest patches, and there is some evidence that mistletoes have increased in the rural districts in south-eastern Australia since the 1900s, especially the box and drooping mistletoes. The box mistletoe is abundant in the central north of New South Wales west of the divide and causes more tree deaths than do other species. They can infest many trees and kill them, further reducing the forests, and they have a detrimental effect on the honey industry. In New Zealand all five remaining native mistletoes have become endangered as a result of browsing by possums.

With the present growing interest in wildlife, ecotourism has become a very popular activity but the impact of tourist activities on the species of interest is rarely considered. A study of rainforest ringtails found that the number of sightings in regularly visited locations had declined. Spotlights are restricted to a maximum of 55 watts but even this level of light caused stress to the possums. Bright light temporarily destroys the night-adapted vision of a possum, which then takes half an hour to return. This happens during the important time for feeding. Under less intense light the rainforest possums made fewer agitated movements and tourists could watch them for longer before they moved off. More individuals were observed, suggesting that they were turning away from the brighter lights.

Pest management

All possums are protected throughout Australia but in Tasmania there is an open season during which Common Brushtail Possums may be harvested under licence for 10 weeks each year and some nuisance animals may be taken under permit.

There are some circumstances in which large possums have become a problem for agriculture and forestry. This is almost entirely the Common Brushtail Possum, but the Mountain Brushtail Possum has also been blamed for tree damage in pine plantations and Common Ringtail Possums may occasionally be a minor pest in orchards. In South Australia 6080 permits were issued for the destruction of Common Brushtail Possums in 1995. These were mostly for possums on Kangaroo Island where they are blamed for widespread agricultural damage.

Possum numbers have increased in the central and south-eastern parts of Tasmania, mostly as a result of the reduction in hunting pressure and land clearing in which a mosaic of pasture and forest is produced. Tasmanian permits are issued only for use on grazing, forestry or farming lands and possums can no longer be trapped using snares. Between 1976 and 1981 more than 250 000 Brushtail Possums were taken annually but since then the price of skins has dropped dramatically and less than 7000 were taken commercially in 1995. Damage of pasture and crops by possums has subsequently increased so the Tasmanian Parks and Wildlife Service now issues many more 'crop protection permits'. The use of the high protein, low fat possum meat is encouraged to supplement the sale of the skins.

Possums damage pine plantations by ringbarking the trees and by topping, (in which the growing tip is broken, causing the main leader to fork into two laterals. Topping can also occur naturally. In the study at Clouds Creek, damage was found to be most severe within 200 metres of the edge of the plantation and closest to the preferred habitat of the Mountain Brushtail Possums. Some small areas sustained a lot of damage to the pine plantations but the overall estimate of possum damage in the plantation was only 4.8 per cent. Other estimates of 63–88 per cent damage by possums to pines were made in the 1950s but it is possible that these estimates did not include an accurate assessment of the actual cause of the damage.

The infectious diseases Bovine Tuberculosis and Leptospirosis are present in New Zealand possum populations and were probably first introduced to the possums from infected livestock. TB was first detected in wild possums in New Zealand in 1970 — it is not known from possums in Australia — and it has now been found in at least 27 widely scattered general localities covering some 13 per cent of the country. This is a significant problem for the livestock industry because the possums constantly reinfect pastures with Bovine Tuberculosis while the New Zealand farmers are attempting to eradicate the disease from their cattle herds.

The control of Common Brushtail Possums in New Zealand is a major industry. Because of Bovine Tuberculosis and the destructive impact of possums on native forests and pine plantations, more time and money has been spent on eradicating the Common Brushtail than on any other pest species in that country. A large body of research has been published about the biology of the species in New Zealand, in order to better understand it and to find more effective control methods. Recently this has included an investigation of reproductive control using immunocontraception as well as a continued assessment of more efficient methods of poisoning.

FURTHER READING

General references and Chapter 1

Flannery, TF (1994) *Possums Of The World,* Geo Productions in Association with the Australian Museum, Sydney.

Fleay, David (1947) *Gliders of the Gum Trees,* Bread and Cheese Club, Melbourne.

Gould, J. (1864) Volume 1 *Mammals of Australia,* Republished 1974 as *Australian Marsupials and Monotremes* with modern commentaries by Joan Dixon, Doubleday & Co, New York.

Lee, AK & Cockburn, A (1985) *Evolutionary Ecology of Marsupials,* Monographs on Marsupial Biology, Cambridge University Press, Melbourne.

McKay, GM (1988) Phalangeridae and Petauridae pp 81–97 In *Zoological Catalogue of Australia*, Vol 5 Mammalia. Bureau of Flora and Fauna, AGPS Canberra.

McKay, GM (1989) Petauridae pp 665–78 In *Fauna of Australia*, Vol 1B. *Mammalia,* (eds Walton, DW & Richardson, BJ), AGPS Canberra.

McKay, GM & Winter, JW (1989) Phalangeridae pp 636–51 In *Fauna of Australia* Vol 1B *Mammalia*, (eds Walton, DW & Richardson, BJ), AGPS Canberra.

Menkhorst, P (ed.) (1995) *Mammals of Victoria, Distribution, Ecology and Conservation,* Oxford University Press, Melbourne.

Montague, T (ed) (2000) *Possums in New Zealand. The Biology, Impact and Management of an Introduced Marsupial,* Manaaki Whenua Press, New Zealand.

Russell, R (1980). *Spotlight on Possums,* University of Queensland Press, Brisbane.

Smith, AP and Hume ID (1984) (eds) *Possums and Gliders,* Surrey Beatty & Sons and the Australian Mammal Society, Sydney. [Many papers from this volume have been referenced extensively but are not listed individually here.]

Smith, MJ (1980) *Marsupials of Australia,* Vol. 1 *Possums, the Koala and Wombats,* Landsdowne Editions, Melbourne.

Strahan, R (1995) *The Mammals of Australia*, Reed Books, Sydney.
Troughton Ellis Le G (1941) *Furred Animals of Australia* Angus and Robertson Ltd, Sydney.
Tyndale-Biscoe, Hugh. (1973) *Life of Marsupials,* Edward Arnold, London.
Tyndale-Biscoe, CH (1981) Advances in marsupial biology — a review of 25 years' research. *Proc. First Symposium on Marsupials in New Zealand* Zool. Publ. from Victoria University, No. 74.
Wood Jones, F, *The Mammals of South Australia*, Government Printer South Australia, 1923–25.

Chapter 2

Fairbairn, Anne (1983) *Shadows of our Dreaming, A celebration of early Australia* Angus and Robertson, Aust.
Heinson, T (1998) Captive Ecology, *Nature Australia* 26(2): 35–43.
Johnson, V (1994) *The Art of Clifford Possum Tjapaltjarri* Craftsman House, Sydney.
Jones, M. (1984) *A Man Called Possum* Published by S. M. Jones, Box 494, Renmark, S.A.
Mulvaney, DJ and White, JP (1987) (eds) *Australians to 1788* Fairfax, Syme and Weldon Associates, Sydney.
Tunbridge, Dorothy (1989) *The Story of the Flinders Ranges Mammals,* Kangaroo Press, NSW.
Turner, Margaret-Mary (1994) *Arrente Foods, Foods from Central Australia,* IAD Press, Alice Springs.

Chapter 3

Archer, M (1987) (ed) *Possums and Opossums: Studies in Evolution*, 2 volumes Surrey Beatty & Sons and the Royal Zoological Society of NSW, Sydney.
Archer, M, Hand, S & Godthelp, H (1991) *Riversleigh*, Reed, Sydney.
Archer, M, Black, K & Nettle, K (1997) Giant Ringtail Possums (Marsupialia, Pseudocheiridae) and Giant Koalas (Phascolarctidae) from the Late Cainozoic of Australia, *Proc. Linn. Soc. NSW* 117: 3–16.
Bassarova, M & Archer, M (1999) Living and extinct Pseudocheirids (Marsupialia, Pseudocheiridae): phylogenetic relationships and changes in diversity through time, *Australian Mammalogy* 21: 25–27.
Crosby, K, Godthelp, H, Archer, A & Pledge, N (1999) Diversity and evolution of Phalangerid, Ektopodontid, Miralinid and Pilkipildrid marsupials, *Australian Mammalogy* 21: 22–23.
Edwards, D & Westerman, M (1995) The molecular relationships of possum and glider families as revealed by DNA–DNA hybridisations, *Aust. J. Zool.* 43: 231–40.
Gemmell, RT & Cepon, G (1993) The development of thermoregulation in the marsupial Brushtail Possum *Trichosurus vulpecula*, *Comp. Biochem. Physiol.* 106A: 167–73.
Haight, JR & Murray, PF (1981) The cranial endocast of the early Miocene marsupial, *Wynyardia bassiana*: an assessment of taxonomic relationships based upon comparisons with recent forms, *Brain, Behav, Evol.* 19: 17–36.
Haight, JR & Neylon, L (1978) Morphological variation in the brain of the marsupial Brush-tailed Possum, *Trichosurus vulpecula, Brain. Behav. Evol.* 15: 415–45.
Johnson-Murray, JL (1987) The comparative myology of the gliding membranes of *Acrobates, Petauroides* and *Petaurus* contrasted with the cutaneous myology of *Hemibelideus* and *Pseudocheirus* (Marsupialia : Phalangeridae) and with selected gliding Rodentia (Scuridae and Anamoluridae), *Aust. J. Zool.* 35:101–13.
Vickers-Rich, P & Rich, TH (1993) *Wildlife of Gondwana,* Reed, Sydney.

Chapter 4

Refer also to papers and species accounts in Strahan (1995) and Smith & Hume (1984)

Calaby, JH (1957) A new record of the Scaly-tailed Possum (*Wyulda squamicaudata* Alexander), *Western Australian Naturalist* 5:186–91.

Dahl, K (1926) *In Savage Australia, An Account of a Hunting and Collecting Expedition to Arnhem Land and Dampier Land,* Philip Allan & Co. London.

George, GG (1987) Characterisation of the living species of Cuscus (Marsupialia: Phalangeridae) pp 507–26, In *Possums and Opossums: studies in evolution* (ed M. Archer), Surrey Beatty & Sons and the Royal Zoological Society of New South Wales, Sydney.

Kerle, JA, McKay GM and Sharman GB (1991) A systematic analysis of the Brushtail Possum, *Trichosurus vulpecula* (Kerr 1792) (Marsupialia : Phalangeridae), *Aust. J. Zool.* 39: 313–31.

Lindenmayer, DB, Viggers, KL, Cunningham, RB and Donnelly, CF (1995) Morphological variation among populations of the Mountain Brushtail Possum, *Trichosurus caninus* Ogilby (Phalangeridae : Marsupialia), *Aust. J. Zool.* 43: 449–58.

McKay GM (1982) Nomenclature of the Gliding Possum genera *Petaurus* and *Petauroides* (Marsupialia : Petauridae), *Aust Mammalogy* 5: 37–39.

Strahan, R (1981) *A Dictionary of Australian Mammal Names* Angus and Robertson, Sydney.

Triggs, B (1996) *Tracks, Scats and Other Traces. A Field Guide to Australian Mammals,* Oxford University Press, Melbourne.

CHAPTER 5

Augee, M, Smith, B & Rose, S (1996) Survival of wild and hand-reared Ringtail Possums (*Pseudocheirus peregrinus*) in bushland near Sydney, *Wildlife Research* 23: 99–108.

Barnett, JL, How, RA & Humphreys, WF (1976) Mammals of Clouds Creek, north-eastern New South Wales, and their distribution in pine and native forests, *The Australian Zoologist* 19: 23–34.

Barnett, JL, How, RA & Humphreys, WF (1979) Blood parameters in natural populations of *Trichosurus* species (Marsupialia : Phalangeridae) II. Influence of habitat and population strategies of *T. caninus* and *T. vulpecula, Aust. J. Zool.* 27: 972–38.

Barnett, JL, How, RA & Humphreys, WF (1982) Habitat effects on organ weights, longevity and reproduction in the Mountain Brushtail Possum, *Trichosurus caninus* (Ogilby), *Aust. J. Zool.* 30: 23–32.

Bennett, AF, Lumsden, LF, Alexander, JSA, Duncan, PE, Johnson, PG, Robertson, P and Silveira, CE (1991) Habitat use by arboreal mammals along an environmental gradient in north-eastern Victoria, *Wildlife Research* 18: 125–46.

Braithwaite, LW (1983) Studies on the arboreal marsupial fauna of eucalypt forests being harvested for woodpulp at Eden, N.S.W. I The species and distribution of animals, *Australian Wildlife Research* 10: 219–30.

Calaby, JH (1966) Mammals of the upper Richmond and Clarence Rivers, New South Wales. *Division of Wildlife Research Technical Paper No. 10* CSIRO, Australia.

Comport, SS, Ward, SJ & Foley, WJ (1996) Home ranges, time budgets and food-tree use in a high density tropical population of Greater Gliders, *Petauriodes volans minor* (Pseudocheiridae : Marsupialia), *Wildlife Research* 23: 401–20.

Davey, SM (1984) Habitat preferences of arboreal marsupials within a coastal forest in southern New South Wales, pp 509–16, In *Possums and Gliders* (eds Smith AP and Hume ID) Surrey Beatty & Sons and the Australian Mammal Society, Sydney.

Driessen, MM, Taylor, RJ & Hocking, GJ (1991) Trends in abundance of three marsupial species after fire, *Australian Mammalogy* 14: 121–24.

Goldingay, R & Daly, G (1997) Surveys of arboreal and terrestrial mammals in the montane forests of Queanbeyan, New South Wales, *Australian Mammalogy* 20: 9–20.

Green, RH (1973) *The Mammals of Tasmania,* Queen Victoria Museum, Launceston, Tasmania.

Green, WQ & Coleman, JD (1987) Den sites of possums, *Trichosurus vulpecula,* and frequency of use in mixed hardwood forest in Westland, New Zealand, *Australian Wildlife Research* 14: 285–92.

Hocking, GJ (1981) The population ecology of the Brushtailed Possum, *Trichosurus vulpecula* (Kerr) in Tasmania, M Sc Thesis, University of Tasmania.

How, RA & Hillcox, S (2000) Brushtail Possum, *Trichosurus vulpecula*, populations in south-western Australia: demography, diet and conservation status, *Wildlife Research* 27: 81–89.

Inions, GB, Tanton, MT & Davey, SM (1989) Effect of fire on the availability of tree hollows used by the Common Brushtail Possum, *Trichosurus vulpecula* Kerr, 1792, and the Ringtail Possum, *Pseudocheirus peregrinus* Boddaerts, 1785, *Australian Wildlife Research* 16: 449–58.

Jones, BA, How, RA & Kitchener, DJ (1994) A field study of *Pseudocheirus occidentalis* (Marsupialia : Petauridae), I. Distribution and habitat, *Australian Wildlife Research* 21: 17–88.

Jones, BA & Hillcox, S (1995) A survey of the possums *Trichosurus vulpecula* and *Pseudocheirus occidentalis* and their habitats in forest at Ludlow, Western Australia, *The Western Australian Naturalist* 20: 139–50.

Kerle, JA (1985) Habitat preference and diet of the Northern Brushtail Possum *Trichosurus arnhemensis* in the Alligator Rivers Region, NT, *Proc. Ecol. Soc. Aust.* 13: 161–76.

Lindenmayer, DB, Cunningham, RB, Donnelly, CF, Triggs, BJ & Belvedere, M (1994) The conservation of arboreal marsupials in the montane ash forests of the central highlands of Victoria, south-east Australia. V. Patterns of use and the microhabitat requirement requirements of the Mountain Brushtail Possum, *Trichosurus caninus* Ogilby in retained linear strips (wildlife corridors), *Biological Conservation* 68: 43–51.

Munks, SA, Corkrey, R and Foley, WJ (1996) Characteristics of arboreal marsupial habitat in the semi-arid woodlands of northern Queensland, *Wildlife Research* 23: 185–96.

Thompson, JA & Owen, WH (1964) A field study of the Australian ringtail possum *Pseudocheirus peregrinus* (Marsupialia : Phalangeridae). *Ecological Monographs* 34: 27–52.

CHAPTER 6

Chilcott, MJ (1984) Coprophagy in the Common Brushtail Possum, *Pseudocheirus peregrinus*. (Marsupialia : Petauridae), *Australian Mammalogy* 7: 107–10.

Cork, SJ & Foley, WJ (1991) Digestive and metabolic strategies of arboreal mammalian folivores in relation to chemical defences in temperate and tropical forests, Chapter 8 In *Plant Defences Against Mammalian Herbivory* (eds Palo, RT & Robbins, CT) CRC Press Boca Raton: Florida.

Ellis, M & Jones, B (1992) Observations of captive and wild Western Ringtail Possums *Pseudocheirus occidentalis, The Western Australian Naturalist* 19: 1–10.

Evans, MC (1992) Diet of the Brushtail Possum *Trichosurus vulpecula* (Marsupialia : Phalangeridae) in central Australia, *Australian Mammalogy* 15: 25–30.

Foley, WJ & Hume, ID (1987) Passage of digesta markers in two species of arboreal folivorous marsupials–the Greater Glider (*Petauroides volans*) and the Brushtail Possum (*Trichosurus vulpecula*), *Physiol. Zool.* 60: 103–113.

Hume ID (1999) *Marsupial Nutrition*, Cambridge University Press, Melbourne.

Kavanagh, RP & Lambert, MJ (1990) Food selection by the Greater Glider, *Petauriodes volans*: is foliar nitrogen a determinant of habitat quality? *Australian Wildlife Research* 17: 285–99.

King, DR, Oliver, AJ & Mead, RJ (1978) The adaptation of some western Australian mammals to food plants containing fluoroacetate, *Aust. J. Zool.* 26: 699–712.

Pahl, LI (1987) Feeding behaviour and diet of the Common Ringtail Possum, *Pseudocheirus peregrinus*, in a *Eucalyptus* woodland and a *Leptospermum* thickets in southern Victoria, *Aust. J. Zool.*, 35: 487–506.

Van Dyck, S (1979) Destruction of wild tobacco trees (*Solanum mauritianum* Scopoli) by Mountain Possums (*Trichosurus caninus* Ogilby), *Mem. Qld. Mus.* 19: 367–71.

Wellard, GA & Hume, ID (1981) Nitrogen metabolism and nitrogen requirements of the Brushtail Possum, *Trichosurus vulpecula* (Kerr), *Aust. J. Zool.* 29: 147–56.

Wellard, GA & Hume, ID (1981) Digesta and digesta passage the Brushtail Possum, *Trichosurus vulpecula* (Kerr), *Aust. J. Zool.* 29:157–66.

CHAPTER 7

Armati-Gulson, P & Lowe, J (1984) The development of the reproductive system of the Common Ringtail Possum, *Pseudocheirus peregrinus* (Marsupialia : Petauridae), *Australian Mammalogy* 7: 75–88.

Bell, BD (ed) (1981) Proceedings of the first symposium on marsupials in New Zealand. Zoology Publications from Victoria University of Wellington Number 74.

Gemmel, RT & Hendrikz, JK (1993) Growth rates of the bandicoot *Isoodon macrourus* and the Brushtail Possum *Trichosurus vulpecula*, *Aust, J. Zool.* 41: 141–49.

How, RA (1976) Reproduction, growth and survival of young in the Mountain Brushtail Possum, *Trichosurus caninus* (Marsupialia), *Aust. J. Zool.* 24: 189–99.

How, RA (1981) Population parameters of two congeneric possums *Trichosurus* spp., in northeastern New South Wales, *Aust. J. Zool.* 29: 205–15.

Hughes, RL & Hall, LS (1984) Embryonic development in the Common Brushtail Possum *Trichosurus vulpecula* pp 197?212, In *Possums and Gliders* (eds Smith AP and Hume ID) Surrey Beatty & Sons and the Australian Mammal Society, Sydney.

Hughes, RL, Thomson, JA & Owen, WH (1965) Reproduction in natural populations of the Australian Ringtail Possum, *Pseudocheirus peregrinus* (Marsupialia : Phalangeridae), in Victoria, *Aust. J. Zoology* 13: 383–406.

Jones, BA, How, RA & Kitchener, DJ (1994) A field study of *Pseudocheirus occidentalis* (Marsupialia : Petauridae), II. Population studies, *Australian Wildlife Research* 21: 189–202.

Kerle, JA & Howe, CJ (1992) The breeding biology of a tropical possum, *Trichosurus vulpecula arnhemensis* (Phalangeridae : Marsupialia), *Aust. J. Zool.* 40: 653–65.

Lyne, AG, Pilton, PE & Sharman, GB (1959) Oestrus cycle, gestation period and parturition in the marsupial *Trichosurus vulpecula*, *Nature* 183: 622–23.

Munks, SA (1990) Ecological energetics and lactation in the Common Ringtail Possum, *Pseudocheirus peregrinus*, *Australian Mammal Society Newsletter* Autumn 1990.

Munks, SA & Green, B (1997) Milk consumption and growth in a marsupial arboreal folivore, the Common Ringtail Possum, *Pseudocheirus peregrinus*, *Physiol. Zool.* 70: 691–700.

Pahl, LI (1987) Survival, age determination and population age structure of the Common Ringtail Possum, *Pseudocheirus peregrinus*, in a *Eucalyptus* woodland and a *Leptospermum* thicket in southern Victoria, *Aust. J. Zool.* 35: 625–39.

Pahl, LI & Lee, AK (1988) Reproductive traits of two populations of the Common Ringtail Possum, *Pseudocheirus peregrinus*, in Victoria, *Aust, J. Zool.* 36: 83–97.

Pilton, PE & Sharman, GB (1962) Reproduction in the marsupial *Trichosurus vulpecula*, *J. Endocrin.* 25: 119–36.

Sharman, GB (1962) The initiation and maintenance of lactation in the marsupial, *Trichosurus vulpecula*, *J. Endocrin* 25: 375–85.

Smith, MJ (1973) Reproduction in the Mountain Brushtail Possum, *Trichosurus caninus* (Ogilby), in captivity, *Aust. J. Zool.* 21: 321–29.

Smith, RFC (1969) Studies on the marsupial glider *Schoinobates volans*, Kerr. I. Reproduction, *Aust. J. Zool.* 17: 625–36.

Tyndale-Biscoe, H & Renfree, M (1987) *Reproductive Physiology of Marsupials* Cambridge, University Press, London.

Tyndale-Biscoe, CH & Smith, RFC (1969) Studies on the marsupial glider *Schoinobates volans* Kerr. II . Population Structure and regulatory mechanisms, *Journal of Animal Ecology* 38: 637–50.

Ward, SJ (1997) Reproductive strategies of marsupial gliders: are they different to those of possums generally? *Australian Mammal Society Newsletter* Nov 1997 p 18.

CHAPTER 8

Biggins, JG & Overstreet, DH (1978) Aggressive and nonaggressive interactions among captive populations of the Brush-tail Possum, *Trichosurus vulpecula*, (Marsupialia : Phalangeridae), *J. Mammalogy* 59: 149–59.

Dunnet, GM (1964) A field study of local populations of the brush-tailed possum,

Trichosurus vulpecula in eastern Australia, *Proceedings of the Zoological Society of London* 142: 665–95.

Hynes, KL (1995) Does the arboreal Brushtail Possum (*Trichosurus vulpecula*) use trees for scent marking? Newsletter of the Australian Mammal Society, Winter 1995.

Kerle, JA (1998) The population dynamics of a tropical possum *Trichosurus vulpecula arnhemensis* Collett, *Wildlife Research* 25: 171–81.

Laurance, WF (1990). Effects of weather on marsupial folivore activity in a north Queensland upland tropical rainforest, *Australian Mammalogy* 13: 41–48.

Lindenmayer, DB, Cunningham, RB, Tanton, MT and Nix, HA (1991) Aspects of use of den trees by arboreal and scansorial marsupials inhabiting montane ash forests in Victoria, *Aust. J. Zool.* 39: 57–65.

Lindenmayer, DB, Welsh, A & Donnelly, CF (1998) Use of nest trees by the Mountain Brushtail Possum (*Trichosurus caninus*) (Phalangeridae : Marsupialia), V. Synthesis of studies, *Wildlife Research* 25: 627–34.

MacLennan, DG (1984) The feeding behaviour and activity patterns of the Brushtail Possum, *Trichosurus vulpecula,* in an open eucalypt woodland in southeast Queensland. pp 155–61, In *Possums and Gliders* (eds Smith AP and Hume ID) Surrey Beatty & Sons and the Australian Mammal Society, Sydney.

Ong, P (1990) Male parental care in the Common Ringtail Possum *Pseudocheirus peregrinus* (Boddaert 1785), *Australian Mammal Society Newsletter* Autumn 1990.

Runcie, M (2000) Adventures at Possum Rock, *Nature Australia* 26(8): 30–37.

Salamon, M (1995) Seasonal variations in the sternal scent secretion in the Brushtail Possum (*Trichosurus vulpecula*), *Newsletter of the Australian Mammal Society* Winter 1995.

Winter, JW (1976) The behaviour and social organisation of the Brushtailed Possum (*Trichosurus vulpecula* Kerr), PhD Thesis, University of Queensland, Brisbane.

CHAPTER 9

Baker, L (1996) (ed) *Mingkiri, A natural history of Uluru by the Mutitjulu Community*, IAD Press, Alice Springs.

Barnett, JL How, RA & Humphreys, WF (1977) Possum damage to pine plantations in north-eastern New South Wales, *Aust. For. Res.* 7: 185–95.

Brunner, H & Wallis, LR (1986) Role of predator scat analysis in Australian mammal research, *Victorian Naturalist* 103: 79–87.

Catling, PC (1988) Similarities and contrasts in the diets of foxes, *Vulpes vulpes*, and cats, *Felis catus*, relative to fluctuating prey populations and drought. *Australian Wildlife Research* 15: 307–18.

Coleman, JD (1981) Tuberculosis and the control of possums *Trichosurus vulpecula* — an expensive business, In *Marsupials in New Zealand* (ed Bell, BD) Zoology publications No: 74 from Victoria University, Wellington.

Cowan, PE, Brockie, RE, Smith, RN & Hearfield ME (1997) Dispersal of juvenile brushtail possums, *Trichosurus vulpecula*, after a control operation, *Wildlife Research* 24: 279–88.

Croft, JD & Hone, LJ (1978) The stomach contents of foxes, *Vulpes vulpes*, collected in New South Wales, *Australian Wildlife Research* 5: 85–92.

De Torres, P, Rosier, S & Paine, G (1998) Conservation of the Western Ringtail Possum, *Pseudocheirus occidentalis*: Review of distribution, and translocation of rehabilitated possums, *Newsletter of the Australian Mammal Society* November 1998 p 27.

Frampton, CM, Warburton, B, Henderson, RJ & Morgan, DR (1999) Optimising bait size and 1080 concentration (sodium monofluoracetate) for the control of brushtail possums (*Trichosurus vulpecula*), *Wildlife Research* 26: 53–60.

Gibbons, P & Lindenmayer, DB (1997) Conserving hollow-dependent fauna in timber-production forests, *Environmental Heritage Monograph Series No* 3, forest issues 2: NSW NPWS.

Gresser, SM, Dickman, CR & Newsome, AE (1997) Outfoxing the fox: Risk-sensitive behaviour in the Common Brushtail Possum, Newsletter of the Australian Mammal Society November 1997.

Kavanagh, RP (1988) The impact of predation by the powerful owl, *Ninox strenua*, on a population of the Greater Glider, *Petauroides volans*, *Aust. J. Ecol.* 13: 445–50.

Kerle, JA, Foulkes, JN, Kimber, RG & Papenfus, D (1992) The decline of the Brushtail Possum, *Trichosurus vulpecula* (Kerr 1798), in arid Australia, *Rangel. J.* 14: 107–27.

Lacy, RC & Lindenmayer, DB (1995) A simulation study of the impacts of population subdivision on the Mountain Brushtail Possum *Trichosurus caninus* Ogilby (Phalangeridae : Marsupialia) in south-eastern Australia. II Loss of genetic variation within and between subpopulations *Biological Conservation* 73: 131–42.

Lavazanian, E, Wallis, R & Webster, A (1994) Diet of Powerful Owls (*Ninox strenua*) living near Melbourne, Victoria, *Wildlife Research* 21: 643–46.

Lindenmayer, DB (1998) *The Design of Wildlife Corridors in Wood Production Forests* NSW National Parks and Wildlife Service, Hurstville NSW.

Lindenmayer, DB, Cunningham, RB & Donnelly, CF (1997) Tree decline and collapse in Australian forests: implications for arboreal marsupials, *Ecological Applications* 7: 625–41.

Lindenmayer, DB & Lacy, RC (1995) Using Population Viability Analysis (PVA) to explore the impacts of population sub-division on the Mountain Brushtail Possum *Trichosurus caninus* Ogilby (Phalangeridae: Marsupialia) in south-eastern Australia, I Demographic stability and population persistence, *Biological Conservation* 73: 119–29.

Lunney, D (1987) Effects of logging, fire and drought on possums and gliders in the coastal forests near Bega, NSW. *Australian Wildlife Research* 14: 263–74

Paton, JB, Alexander, PJ, Bird, PL, Dal Piva, F, Inns, RW, Kellty DK and Storr, RF (1997) *The Common Brushtail Possum In South Australia*, Seminar Proceedings, Fauna Management Co-ordinating Committee NPW, SA.

Pietsch, RS (1995) The fate of urban Common Brushtail Possums translocated to sclerophyll forest. pp 239–46, In *Reintroduction Biology of Australian and New Zealand Fauna* (ed Serena, M) Surrey Beatty & Sons, Sydney.

Presidente, PJA, Barnett, JL, How, RA & Humphreys, WF (1982) Effects of habitat, host sex and age on the parasites of *Trichosurus caninus* (Marsupialia : Phalangeridae) in north-eastern New South Wales, *Aust. J. Zool.* 30: 33–47.

Runcie, M (1998) Management considerations of two species of rock-dwelling possum, *Newsletter of the Australian Mammal Society* November 1998, p27.

Seebeck, JH (1977) Mammals in the Melbourne metropolitan area, *Victorian Naturalist* 94: 165–71.

Smith, B (1995) *Caring for Possums,* Kangaroo Press Pty Ltd, Sydney.

Statham, M & Statham, HL (1997) Movements and habits of brushtail possums (*Trichosurus vulpecula*) in an urban area, *Australian Wildlife Research* 24: 715–26.

Tasmanian Parks and Wildlife Service (1996) Management program for the Brushtail Possum *Trichosurus vulpecula* Kerr in Tasmania–review of background information, URL: www.environment.gov.au/bg/plants/wildlife/posmindx.htm

Tilley, S (1982) The diet of the Powerful Owl, *Ninox strenua*, in Victoria, *Australian Wildlife Research* 9:157–75.

Triggs, B, Brunner, H & Cullen, JM (1984) The food of fox, cat and dog in Croajingalong National Park, south-eastern Victoria, *Australian Wildlife Research* 11: 491–500.

Tyndale-Biscoe, CH & Smith, RFC (1969) Studies on the marsupial glider *Schoinobates volans* Kerr. III. Response to habitat destruction, *Journal of Animal Ecology* 38: 651–59.

Viggers, KL & Spratt, DM (1995) The parasites recorded from *Trichosurus* species (Marsupialia: Phalangeridae), *Wildlife Research* 22:311–32.

Wilson, R (1999) Possums in the spotlight, *Nature Australia* 26(4): 34–41.

Winter, JW (1979) The status of endangered Australian Phalangeridae, Petauridae, Burramyidae, Tarsipedidae and the Koala, Ch 4 In *The status of endangered Australasian Wildlife* (ed Tyler, M), *Proc. Royal Society S. A.*

Wood, MS & Wallis, RL (1998) Potential competition for nest sites between feral European Honeybees (*Apis mellifera*) and Common Brushtail Possums (*Trichosurus vulpecula*), *Australian Mammalogy* 20:377–81.

INDEX

Italic page numbers refer to illustrations